STRENGTH THROUGH GENERATIONS

Strength Through Generations

A Black American Family's Fight for Equality Through Faith, Love, and Education

Percy Brown, Jr.

©2025 All Rights Reserved. No portion of this book may be reproduced, stored in a retrieval system, or transmitted in any form or by any means—electronic, mechanical, photocopy, recording, scanning, or other—except for brief quotations in critical reviews or articles without the prior permission of the author.

Published by Game Changer Publishing

Paperback ISBN: 978-1-966659-67-9

Hardcover ISBN: 978-1-966659-68-6

Digital ISBN: 978-1-966659-69-3

www.GameChangerPublishing.com

DEDICATION

I dedicate this book to the Brown family, past and present. Your unwavering support and love have been the bedrock of my life, shaping me into the person I am today. Thank you for always being there for me.

I dedicate this book to my wife, Carissa, and daughter, Jordyn. Your constant encouragement and belief in me have been my guiding light, pushing me to strive for excellence and reach for the stars.

I dedicate this book to the late Rev. Dr. Allen Dennis and Bruce Dahmen, my white American brothers, who saw something in me before I saw it in myself.

I dedicate this book to the late Rev. Richard Jones, Sr., for believing in me and fighting for me to become the educator I am today.

I dedicate this book to the thousands of young people I have inspired, and who in return, have inspired me.

READ THIS FIRST

Just to say thanks for buying and reading my book,
I would like to give you access to valuable resources and
an invitation to free virtual talkbacks with me!

STRENGTH THROUGH GENERATIONS

A BLACK AMERICAN FAMILY'S FIGHT FOR EQUALITY THROUGH FAITH, LOVE, AND EDUCATION

PERCY BROWN, JR.

FOREWORD

Everyone likes a good story. Narratives are not merely about making people feel good but rather about helping us make sense of ourselves and our place in the world. In many African nations, the person who is the keeper of the community stories is known as the *griot*. People in these roles are given special training from childhood to teach them how to remember the people's stories. Indeed, in some societies—Indigenous people of the Americas, Native Hawaiian peoples of the South Pacific, Akan, Ibo, Dogon, Xosa, Kikuyu people of the continent of Africa—human beings cannot exist "outside" of the community and cultural story. The story validates your very existence.

In 1977, author Alex Haley (best known for his *Autobiography of Malcolm X*) permitted the book based on his own family's life, *Roots*, to be serialized and broadcast on the ABC television network. For 8 nights, a record number of Americans sat glued to their television screens to watch the story of ONE family. It was an unusual story of a Black family because it traces its origins back to the African continent—something most Americans of African ancestry cannot do. The brutality of the European slave trade in Africa systematically erased the personal and cultural identities of most enslaved people. By eradicating their native languages, religions, customs, traditions, and cultures, these people were forced to create new narratives forged in the Americas and bereft of their African identities and cultural knowledge.

I am only able to trace my family's stories back to about the 1830s, when my maternal great-great-grandparents, Peter and Lena Trapp, both victims of the brutality of slavery in Fairfield County, South Carolina, did their best to keep their family intact and maintain their humanity amongst the most inhumane of systems. However, even without a definitive origin story from Africa, I do have a captivating story. My parents on both sides are from South Carolina, the site of the largest embarkation of Africans to these shores. Over 40 percent of Black people entered the U.S. via Charleston, South Carolina. My family—my mother's and father's lines—originated in South Carolina. In fact, my maiden name, Ladson, is the name of a census-designated place just outside of Charleston, Berkeley, and Dorchester Counties, South Carolina. The name is in honor of one of the oldest planter families in the Charleston area, the Ladson Family, whose member, James Ladson, was the state's lieutenant governor. Interestingly, my father's name was James Ladson.

My mother's side, the Woodwards, may have descended from Robert Woodward Barnwell, who went on to be a U.S. congressman and later a Confederate senator. His family was one of the wealthy planters and slavers in the state who reportedly "owned"[1] 126 enslaved people of African descent. However, I have less documentation to prove this. I do know that my grandparents

---

1. I have placed the word "owned" in quotation marks to signal my resistance to the notion that human beings can be owned.

on both sides were sharecroppers. The sharecropping system was a brutally unfair way to extract labor from poor farmers without compensating them. It was the major way formerly enslaved people could make a living. They remained on the land of previous plantations and small farms, worked the land, and paid a portion of their harvest to the landowner. The problem was the sharecropper had to purchase all of his supplies, seeds, and equipment from the landowner. By the time the accounts were settled, the sharecropper with little or no schooling was in no position to dispute the accounting and found himself and his family further in debt. It was an impossible system in which no sharecropper could ever get ahead. It was just one step away from slavery.

My maternal grandfather escaped the horror of the sharecropping system by obtaining a job as a stevedore on the Pennsylvania Railroad. He brought his wife and his five children to Philadelphia, where they settled, had two additional children, and lived out the rest of their lives. My paternal grandfather never left South Carolina, but six of his seven children eventually made their way to Philadelphia. My father, at 12 years old, accompanied his 14-year-old brother by walking, hitchhiking, and jumping freight trains north to Philadelphia. The stories on both sides of my family were constant reminders of the ongoing hope and sense of determination that were a part of what would make me who I am.

In Philadelphia, my parents suffered from what is known as *de facto* segregation. While the laws in the North did not explicitly deny my parents some services, the customs regularly reinforced a system of discrimination that meant my mother could not try on garments in downtown department stores before purchasing them. My father was prohibited from purchasing a home in suburban Philadelphia because of covenants and deed restrictions, and we lived in a community where almost all of the children with whom I attended school were Black.

However, my parents were resourceful and realized that while sitting beside white children would not make me smarter, money followed white children. As my mother once told me, "They don't have to be happy about your being there. It is impossible for them to teach 'around' you. You can learn whatever they're teaching." That perspective is what had my mother maneuver to get her children into schools across town in White middle-class neighborhoods once we completed our education at our all-Black elementary school.

The advantage of that elementary school was that it exposed me to Black teachers who invested in Black children. I learned Black history in 5th grade and heard about people like W. E. B. DuBois, Booker T. Washington, Mary Church Terrell, Ida B. Wells, Anna Julia Cooper, Mary McLeod Bethune, and many others. These names were not repeated when I attended mostly white junior and senior high schools. I did not hear of them in a school setting until I chose to attend a Historically Black College/University (HBCU) in Maryland. Of course, I did receive some knowledge of Black history and culture as a regularly attending member of a Black church and at my family's dinner table. However, my college experience gave me the opportunity to study under the direction of brilliant historians. I learned and recaptured the "stories" of the Black American sojourn in the Americas as well as on the continent of Africa.

The most important experience of my undergraduate years may have been the ability to actively participate in the modern Civil Rights Movement. My college years were bookended by the assassinations of Malcolm X and Martin Luther King, Jr. I regularly participated in marches and protests on issues such as housing, jobs, and equal rights. I picketed outside of retail stores that refused to serve Black people and marched in neighborhoods that harassed Black residents. I attended mass rallies and public meetings with speakers and artists like Stokely Carmichael (Kwame Toure), Muhammad Ali, and Nina Simone. My cultural and political education was enhanced by attending a college that addressed my needs and urged us to engage in social and political activism.

After serving as a public school teacher, I returned to graduate school and eventually earned a PhD from one of the nation's most prestigious universities. My preparation at an HBCU stood me in good stead and made me competitive in classes against peers who had received their education at Ivy League, private liberal arts, and research-intensive state land-grant schools. My career as an academic flourished and eventually earned me the distinction of being the first Black woman to earn tenure in a School of Education that existed since 1848. I also became an endowed professor, president of two education research organizations, and holder of nine honorary degrees.

I share these accolades not as a way to uplift myself but to point out the importance of the enduring spirit of my parents, my grandparents, my great-grandparents, and my great-great-grandparents to persevere despite the odds. Like the book you are about to read, they represented "strength through generations." I also include my story as a way to demonstrate that people find ways to persevere in the face of many obstacles. And finally, I share my story as a way to remind each of us that we have generational stories to reflect upon and to tell our children and our grandchildren so they will recognize the ways their generations have strengthened them.

~ Gloria Ladson-Billings
Madison, Wisconsin

CONTENTS

READ THIS FIRST	1
FOREWORD	5
INTRODUCTION	13
CHAPTER 1	19
CHAPTER 2	33
CHAPTER 3	47
CHAPTER 4	61
CHAPTER 5	107
CHAPTER 6	123
CHAPTER 7	137
CONCLUSION	155
SELF REFLECTIVE ACTIVITIES	165
THANK YOU FOR READING MY BOOK!	167

INTRODUCTION

*"Turning nothing into something is God's work.
And you get nothing without struggle and hard work."*
~Nas

The United States is one of the most diverse nations on earth. The students in our schools reflect this diversity, while the teaching force does not share the exact reflection. For example, Black students account for 21% of public school students, while Black teachers make up 6.1% of the teaching force nationally. Black male educators account for 2% of the nation's teaching force, and I fall into that category. I have over two decades of experience working in public schools and institutions of higher learning. Embedding Black history into social studies courses in public education is why I got into education. For the past 20 years, I have been able to teach Black history to thousands of students in informal ways and by speaking at school assemblies during Black History Month. However, I have failed to incorporate Black history into a social studies curriculum. I have spent the last 12 years leading diversity, equity, and inclusion work in two predominantly white, affluent school districts in Wisconsin. Two years ago, a student shared that she was enrolled in an online African American history course because we did not offer it at the high school. I had an opportunity to review the course materials and was disappointed. It credited Africa as the birthplace of humanity. What followed was a picture of Charles Darwin and his theory of evolution. I was baffled to see an image of Charles Darwin and his theory of evolution in an African American history course. While subliminal, if one does not know the history of race, they will not be able to see it perpetuates the perception of racial inferiority.

Furthermore, the first image you see of a Black person in the course is in chains because it skips over ancient African civilizations and goes straight to the enslavement of Black people. I brought this to the attention of the district e-school principal, Jill Gurtner, and we decided to do something about it. We began working together to build an African American history course for high school students in the district, but we were told that we had to put the project on hold for some reason temporarily.

Being denied that opportunity was disheartening. In addition to being denied a chance to build a Black history course for the high school, I was being attacked by a political think tank in Wisconsin and families from the district who organized to push back on equity efforts across the state and in the district. These groups, who were opposed to the inclusion of Black history in the curriculum, wrote manifestos and had private social media accounts in which they accused me of being a "radical revolutionary and promoting violent revolution." Their opposition was not just about the content of the curriculum but about the very idea of Black history being taught in schools. I met with these families in person and shared with them that my efforts are humanitarian and rooted in faith. I told them I followed the teachings and philosophy of the late Dr. Martin Luther King, Jr. It did not matter what I shared because their minds were made up, and the attacks continued. The weight of leading this work in a predominantly white school district is exhausting due to the nature of the role, forcing you to swim against the current daily. Although I love the work, I would not wish this role on anyone. I was at my breaking point during the 2022-23 school year and almost walked away from working in public schools.

In 1954, the monumental Brown v. Board of Education Supreme Court decision ended racial segregation in schools but did not address the curriculum, which was devoid of Black history. Carter G. Woodson, the father of Black History Month, was a trailblazer on this issue. In 1933 he released a book, *The Mis-Education of the Negro*, and Woodson writes, "No thought was given to the history of Africa except so far as it had been a field of exploitation for the Caucasian. You might study history as it was offered in our system from elementary school throughout the university, and you would never hear Africa mentioned except in the negative." Universities have made progress by adding African American studies to the curriculum and as an option for bachelor's and master's degrees. However, little progress has been made in our K–12 public schools.

In July 2023, along with over 120 Black Americans, I was blessed to travel to Egypt with Tony Browder, a Black American scholar who has written several books on Ancient Kemet (Egypt) and led close to 30, if not more, study tours there for Black Americans. On this trip, Tony challenged the participants to spread their newfound learning in their communities. Moreover, it was more than just the learning we received in Africa. Tony charged us to ensure that Black children in our communities learn their history because public school systems across the nation do not do Black history justice.

My journey to Africa was a turning point that inspired me to write this book. With a background in history and political science, my passion for Black history was kindled in my formative years. I was immersed in activism due to my father's family's involvement in the Mississippi Delta civil rights movement. Growing up in a Black church in the Midwest with members who were actively involved in civil rights activism and learning the teachings of Dr. King and Malcolm X in my teen years and twenties, I was steeped in the importance of Black history. The influence of early hip-hop artists, who advocated for Black youths to embrace their history and culture, further shaped my understanding. These personal experiences have shaped my understanding of Black history's importance in education but also fueled my commitment to this cause.

From a young age, I was determined to carry on the legacy of fighting for racial equality, inspired by the activists and leaders around me. This commitment remains unwavering as I continue to advocate for the inclusion of Black history in education. Despite the challenges and attacks I have faced, my resolve has only strengthened. I hope that my resilience in the face of adversity will inspire others to join this crucial fight.

Remember, 21% of students in public schools are Black Americans, and they should have the right to learn about who they are. Most educators have learned about Maslow's Hierarchy of Needs, a theory about the physiological and psychological needs required for all human beings to develop themselves and fully find purpose in their lives. Maslow argues that every human being, particularly children, needs to create a strong sense of self-worth or self-esteem. Based on my understanding of Maslow, the lack of Black history in the curriculum is not just a matter of academic content but a direct assault on the self-esteem of Black children. By limiting Black history to the topic of slavery, public schools are not only hindering their academic growth but also their personal development, as they are denied the opportunity to learn about their rich cultural heritage and the achievements of their ancestors.

As a Black male educator with a background in social studies, I know that America's schools focus heavily on teaching slavery, but this does not address the more significant curricular issue when it comes to the history of Black people. What I mean by that is that not much exists in the curriculum about who Black people were before the transatlantic slave trade. There's no mention of ancient African civilizations, such as the Kingdoms of Mali, Songhai, Benin, Kemet, Nubia, Axum, and Ethiopia. Such a rich history is omitted in our curriculum. I would also argue that parts of slavery were so horrific that most teachers in public schools are not equipped with the skills to teach the subject. I am not saying that slavery should not be taught in public schools. I argue that public schools must teach a more comprehensive history of Black people, particularly the aspects that will build the self-esteem of Black children and change the perception of those who are not Black.

The United States is amid a culture war. We, the people, are becoming tribal and wholly opposed to being around people who do not share our views. At the center of the culture wars that exist is race. I mentioned being called a radical revolutionary. This is a result of politicians and media calling the teachings about race "woke" ideology or critical race theory. This broad generalization serves as a boogeyman to the American mind, and rather than seek truth and understanding, those in power prefer the American mind remain asleep. I am not a race baiter nor someone who pushes a victimization ideology about the experiences of Black people. I am a seeker of truth and understanding. I am faith-based and value family, hard work, love for humanity, compassion, and empathy. I believe that we, the people, are better when we can work together.

The only way to end the culture wars in the nation, specific to race, is for every citizen to consider becoming culturally literate. According to the Metiri Group, to be culturally literate is to be "knowledgeable and appreciative of the way that culture and history—their own as well as the culture of others—impact behaviors, beliefs, and relationships in a multicultural world." The path to cultural literacy is simple: It requires self-reflection and perspective-taking. This book takes the reader on a journey to become culturally literate, using Black history and personal narrative as the foundation for perspective-taking. The title of each chapter is a quote or the name of a speech by historical Black scholars and activists who have influenced my life and served as models of inspiration. Each chapter title aligns with the content of each chapter and serves as additional reading, listening, and perspective. Included at the end of the book are self-reflective activities designed to help you understand more about yourself while learning about Black history and the lived experiences of the Brown family. These activities, alongside the reading of this book, create the conditions for meaningful perspective-taking.

This book is about shifting one's mindset. I ask you to step inside my shoes while learning more about yourself. Malcolm X said, "Ignorance of each other has made unity impossible. We need more light about each other. Light creates understanding, understanding creates love, love creates patience, and patience creates unity. Once we have more knowledge about each other, we will stop condemning each other, and a united front will be brought about."

Unity is the aim of the book and my hope for the future of this nation.

CHAPTER 1

"What to the slave is the Fourth of July?"
~ Frederick Douglass
Speech on July 5, 1852 in Rochester, New York
Overview of the History of Race and
its Influence on Colonial America
and the New Nation through 1865

What is legacy? On my office wall, I have a picture that defines the phrase. It says, *"Legacy is the story you leave behind for others to tell. In other words, it is the impression you make on the next generation. It is not based on money or material things but on character, conviction, and compassion."*

Legacy is history. Legacy is family history. Legacy is doing the work of making the world a better place for the future. Welcome to my world and the legacy of the Brown family.

My great-grandmother's grandfather, Taylor Holden, was

born about 1823, and according to the 1870 U.S. Census data, he had a personal estate of $200, six children, and resided in Ward 6, Natchitoches, Louisiana. I have found documentation showing that the Freedmen's Bureau employed Taylor Holden from 1865 to 1877. My great-grandmother's father, John Holden, was born about 1853 and was the oldest of Taylor's six children. Taylor and John were both farmers and alive while slavery was still legal. However, I have been unable to find out if Taylor and John were enslaved because the Census Bureau only tracked the race and gender of Black people before 1870.

I have learned that the Africans who came to Louisiana, which France colonized, were highly skilled in agriculture, leatherwork, copperwork, Blacksmithing, and hunting. Some were even medically skilled in treating malaria and yellow fever. The Africans in French Louisiana also possessed a strong sense of justice and were not afraid to demand their rights within the framework of slavery. I can safely assume that Taylor Holden was highly skilled in farming if he stayed employed with the Freedmen's Bureau during Reconstruction.

Farming was how my family maintained their way of life for generations. My great-grandfather John Holden was married to Scarlett Holden and had four children. My great-grandmother Eliza, born around 1875, was the oldest of her siblings and grew up in Ward 6, Natchitoches, Louisiana. She later met my great-grandfather Morgan Brown II, and they were married on February 13, 1889. Morgan II was a farmer, and as early as 1910, he and Eliza identified as literate and able to write, as well as owning a farm and a home. They were mortgage-free by 1920 and had 12 children.

Frederick Douglass was born and enslaved on the eastern shores of Maryland around the same time as my great-great-great-grandfather. He escaped slavery, was self-taught, and was the most essential Black leader fighting against slavery in the 19th century. On July 5, 1852, in Rochester, New York, Douglass delivered his speech "What to the Slave is the Fourth of July" to an all-white audience of hundreds. He praised the founders for the ideals of freedom and democracy while chastising them for being hypocritical for enslaving and discriminating against Black people. His speech provides a first-hand account of life being an enslaved and later a free Black person in America. Douglass argues that the nation needs to provide for Black Americans the same rights as whites based on the words, "We hold these truths to be self-evident, that all men are created equal," in the Declaration of Independence. Douglass may not have known that "created equal" did not equate to "born equal" in the minds of the Founding Fathers. There is a difference between the two according to the Laws of Nature, which is mentioned in the Declaration of Independence. In this chapter, I will highlight the origins of race and expose Europeans' justification for enslaving people of African descent through the academic study of natural history or the laws of nature. Moreover, I will show how the study of natural history in Europe influenced the social, political, economic, and overall cultural landscape of the United States.

Culture can be defined in many ways, but for this book, I want to use the definition offered by Sir Edward Burnett Taylor, who is known as the founder of academic anthropology in the English-speaking world and the author of the first anthropology textbook. Taylor defines culture as "a complex whole which includes knowledge, belief, art, morals, law, customs, and any other capabilities and habits acquired by man as a member of society."

Within the complex whole, Taylor embeds "belief" and "laws" as part of what creates a society's culture. In colonial America, there was a deep belief that Black people were inferior to whites. This deep belief manifested itself in the laws and social fabric of the nation. Let us begin in 1789. That is when the Constitutional Convention ratified the United States Constitution, the document that binds us together as United States of America citizens.

The Preamble to the Constitution states, "We, the people of the United States, in order to form a more perfect union, establish justice, ensure domestic tranquility, provide for the common defense, promote the general welfare, and secure the blessings of liberty to ourselves and our posterity, do ordain and establish this Constitution for the United States of America." The Preamble lays out the social fabric of the nation, followed by the Bill of Rights and the structure of government.

The framers of the U.S. Constitution believed in a governmental structure grounded in checks and balances, meaning the government should not be run by a single faction of government, like that of a monarchy. Therefore, the framers formed three branches of government with distributive powers, and they are the legislative, judicial, and executive branches of government. One of the first pieces of legislation Congress passed was the Naturalization Act of 1790. It states: "Be it enacted by the Senate and House of Representatives of the United States of America and Congress assembled that any alien being a free white person who shall have resided within the limits and under the jurisdiction of the United States for the term of two years may be admitted to become a citizen thereof on application to any common law court of record in any one of the states where then he shall reside for the term of one year." With citizenship rights established, the nation began tracking the overall population.

At the time, the nation tracked its white, free Black, and enslaved Black people. Tracking the population by state was needed to determine how many seats each state would receive in the House of Representatives. At the time of the Constitutional Convention, there were five slaveholding states—Virginia, Maryland, South Carolina, North Carolina, and Georgia—that wanted to count their enslaved Blacks as part of their total population. Counting enslaved Blacks as part of the total population of slaveholding states would have dramatically increased their number of seats and power in the House of Representatives. In the spirit of cooperation and a balanced approach to power, what resulted was the Three-Fifths Compromise, which meant that every enslaved African a slaveholding state possessed, they would get three-fifths of that number added to the population of white citizens residing in the state.

The following are approximate numbers of enslaved Africans included in the population by state when the Constitution was ratified. Virginia had 280,000 enslaved Blacks, with Maryland and South Carolina having 80,000 enslaved Blacks. North Carolina had 60,000 enslaved Blacks, and Georgia had 20,000 enslaved Blacks. As you can see, although Black Americans were not first-class citizens, they were still factored into the political infrastructure of the nation.

The population in 1790 was 3,172,006 whites, 59,527 freed Blacks, and 697,681 enslaved Blacks. Blacks comprised 19.3% of the population, with 7.9% free and 92.1% enslaved. By 1860, the white population rose to 26,922,537. That year, there were 488,070 freed Blacks and 3,953,760 enslaved Blacks. Whites made up 85.6% of the population, and Blacks made up 14.1%, with 11% of Blacks being free and 89% being enslaved.[1] 1860 is also the year the Census Bureau included American Indian, Eskimo, and Aleut as one racial classification and Asian and Pacific Islander as another racial classification in tracking the United States racial

---

1. Wright, C. D., & Hunt, W. C. (1900). *The history and growth of the United States Census: Prepared for the Senate Committee on the census.* United States Government Printing Office.

demographic data. More important is the significant growth of enslaved labor that occurred between 1790 and 1860. To understand this explosion, you must understand the way religion and science influenced the system of enslaving Black people.

Concerning religion, I will briefly highlight how the Roman Catholic Church demonized people from Africa centuries before the founding of the United States. Subsequently, I will expose the role 18th- and 19th-century European scholars of natural history played in shaping the beliefs about humanity based on skin color. During the mid-1400s, the Portuguese explored and traded in Africa. Part of the trade included purchasing and exporting Africans to be sold into enslavement in Europe. Earl Conrad, an American author with over 20 published books, wrote a book called *The Invention of the Negro*.

Conrad writes, "Fifty years before Columbus sailed westward, Catholic Spain and Catholic Portugal were engaged in a rivalry to sack Africa to seize its inhabitants as enslaved people and to ship them back to Europe and sell them. Portugal, the first invader, sought and secured the blessings of the Pope. In a series of papal bulls issued from 1443 on, there is a spectacle of the Christian Vatican sanctifying this enslavement of Africans on the grounds that they were pagans."

Here, we have a religious rationale for the sanctioning of the enslavement of Black people. It may not have been about skin color at that time. Still, because Africa was considered uncivilized or not Christianized, the Catholic Church deemed Black people to be pagans, justifying their enslavement by the Portuguese and later the rest of Europe. The religious rationalization for enslaving Black people would eventually manifest itself in academia in Western Europe.

European scholars of natural history were responsible for constructing the concept of categorizing human beings and assigning innate abilities and character traits based on skin color. Their beliefs, rooted in fictive biology, can be defined as scientific racism. Scientific racism is the theory that different racial and ethnic groups have innately different levels of physical, intellectual, and moral development that distinguish them as superior or inferior.

European scholar of natural history, Carl Linnaeus, was the first person to classify human beings. He looked at continents and classified those in Europe as white, the Americas as red, those from Asia as tawny, and Africans as Black. Most scholars pinpoint Carl Linnaeus's work as the root of what would emerge as scientific racism. What followed from Linnaeus's work were other European scholars of natural history who developed the Great Chain of Being or Laws of Nature. This concept placed all living organisms on earth on a hierarchical scale, beginning with God as universal law, followed by natural law, or the laws of nature. For centuries, the study of natural history in Europe disregarded what they knew about humanity and instead pushed a belief that Black people were inherently inferior to them.

The following are belief statements about Black people from some of the most recognized European scholars of natural history during the 18th century.

Scottish philosopher and historian David Hume, who lived from 1711 to 1776, wrote, "I am apt to suspect the Negroes and, in general, all of the other species of men to be naturally inferior to the whites. There never was a civilized nation of any other complexion other than white."

Christoph Meiners, a professor at Gottingen University in the late 18th century, was a German racialist and one of the earlier practitioners of scientific racism He believed that each race had a separate origin. Meiners wrote an article titled "On the Nature of the African Negro." In it, he describes the white race and Europeans as superior based on their beauty compared to all other racial groups, opposes the abolition of slavery, and states that Black people lack virtue and control over their harmful vices.

Johann Blumenbach, one of the most recognized scholars of natural history in the late 18th century, is responsible for how we have come to understand race today. Blumenbach was a student at the University of Göttingen, where he pursued his doctoral studies and wrote his dissertation titled *On the Natural Varieties of Mankind*. Blumenbach, building off of Carolus Linnaeus, divided the human family into five categories: Caucasian, Mongolian, Malay, American Indian, and Negro. This hit academia in 1795, and this construct of humanity is embedded as a category in the collection of United States census data.

Martin Bernal, who wrote the book *Black Athena: The Afro-Asiatic Roots of Greece*, had this to say about Blumenbach in his book: "Blumenbach was the first to publicize the term Caucasian, which he used for the first time in the third edition of his great work the *Generis Humani Varietate Nativa* in 1795. According to him, the white or Caucasian was the first and most beautiful and talented race from which all the others had degenerated to become Chinese, Negroes, etc. Blumenbach justified the curious name Caucasian on scientific and racial grounds."

Pietrus Camper, a Dutch physician, physiologist, and naturalist, believed that ancient Greece and Rome came the closest to achieving a perfect civilization. He was the first scientist to introduce angles and measurements of human skull features as another form of scientific method to prove the racial inferiority of Black people. Camper's work marked the beginning of Europeans exaggerating the skull features of Africans and Asians, using these measurements to determine superiority and inferiority within the human family.

These beliefs were widespread across Europe and colonial

America and influenced legislation that placed Black people into an inferior status socially, politically, and economically. In the 1600s, Britain created laws and policies that designated Blacks as persons of inferior status. This occurred in Colonial America, beginning in the colony of Virginia. On August 20, 1619, the first ship of enslaved Africans to colonial America arrived at Jamestown, Virginia. By 1639, the state of Virginia enacted its first slave codes. One of them read as follows: "Whereas some doubts have arisen whether children got by an Englishman upon a Negro shall be slave or free, be it therefore enacted and declared by this present Grand Assembly that all children born in this country shall be held bond or free only according to the condition of the mother." What this is saying is that regardless of the father's ethnicity, if the mother is Negro and enslaved at the time, her baby would automatically be enslaved. The father did not matter. At this time, it was rare for interracial pregnancies to happen between a Black man and a white woman.

The colony of Virginia also enacted Act X in 1639, and it reads as follows: "All persons except Negroes are to be provided with arms and ammunition or be fined at the pleasure of the governor and council." In 1705, the colony of Virginia passed an additional slave code, which reads as follows: "If any slave resists his master, correcting such a slave, and shall happen to be killed in such correction, the master shall be free of all punishments as any other person whatsoever if such accident never happened." This law offered no protection to enslaved Black people.

If a white person were to kill an enslaved Black person, it was not a violation of the law. It is evident that for more than 100 years before the ratification of the Constitution, laws were passed that restricted Blacks from having the same access and rights as white colonialists, including white indentured servants.

In 1793, the United States further restricted the rights and movements of Black people by passing the Fugitive Slave Act. This Act empowered local communities to capture and return enslaved Africans who had escaped their owners while issuing citations to anyone who may have assisted in the escape. Interestingly, this Act establishes one of the nation's earliest forms of law enforcement. Its sole purpose was to restrict and control only Black people.

The Fugitive Slave Act also came to the detriment of freed Blacks during this time. For example, Solomon Northrup was a freed Black man in the North who found himself in the wrong place at the wrong time. He was captured by fugitive slave catchers and sold into slavery for 12 years. He wrote a book about his experiences, *12 Years a Slave*. In 2013, movie director Steve McQueen released the film version of the book *12 Years a Slave*.

To better understand the manifestation of such policies and what would follow before the Civil War, we must examine the beliefs of two historical figures we praise today. First, Thomas Jefferson was one of the founding fathers of this nation, the third president of the United States, and the author of the Declaration of Independence. Secondly, Abraham Lincoln was the 16th president of the United States and was responsible for ending the enslavement of Black people in the United States. Beginning with Jefferson in the late 1700s, he wrote a book, *Notes on the State of Virginia*, to respond to questions from a British journalist. In this book, Jefferson writes extensively and shares his beliefs about Black people.

Jefferson believed that Blacks and whites could never coexist. He wrote, "Deep-rooted prejudices entertained by the whites, 10,000 recollections by the Blacks of the injuries they have sustained, new provocations, the real distinctions nature has made, and many other circumstances will divide us into parties and produce convulsions which will probably never end but in the extermination of the one race or the other." Jefferson also proposed a repatriation plan for Blacks. He suggested that the United States provide Blacks in the nation everything they needed, including protection, until they could develop a solid independent state for themselves outside of the United States. To make up for that lost labor, he also had an immigration plan—specifically, for white immigrants. He would encourage white people from around the world to immigrate to the United States. Each African that was removed from the country would be replaced by a white immigrant. This was his thinking.

Lastly, Jefferson had the same mindset as the European scholars of natural history I mentioned. Regarding the innate abilities of Black people, Jefferson writes, "To our reproach, it must be said that though for a century and a half, we have had under our eyes the races of Black and red men. They have never yet been viewed by us as subjects of natural history. I advanced it therefore as a suspicion only that the Blacks, whether originally a distinct race or made distinct by circumstance, are inferior to the whites in the endowments of both body and mind."

In 1857, three years before the presidency of Abraham Lincoln, Jefferson's beliefs about Black people were deeply embedded in the cultural landscape of the nation and were reinforced when the United States Supreme Court heard the Dred Scott v. Sandford case. Dred Scott was an enslaved Black man owned by Dr. John Emerson. Emerson was a U.S. Army surgeon who traveled to the free territories of Illinois and Wisconsin for work. Often, Dred Scott would travel to those free territories with Dr. Emerson. While in those territories with Dr. Emerson, Scott was legally free. Scott was aware of this and believed he should be freed because, in his home state of Missouri, where he and Emerson were from, a statute said, "Once free, always free." The United States Supreme Court ruled 8-1 that the Constitution does not extend citizenship, rights, or privileges to Black people. Therefore, the state statute did not apply to him.

One year later, Abraham Lincoln campaigned against Stephen Douglass to represent Illinois as one of its United States Senators. Lincoln and Douglass debated one another and had to respond to questions on the issue of race and slavery. Lincoln, who is recognized for ending slavery in the United States when referring to Blacks during the debate, said, "I have no purpose to introduce political and social equality between the white and Black races. There is a physical difference between the two, which, in my judgment, will probably forever forbid their living together upon the equal footing of perfect equality."

When the Civil War ended, President Lincoln, like President Jefferson, had a repatriation plan for newly freed Blacks. Thousands of newly freed Blacks participated in this plan and returned to Africa, where they established the country of Liberia.

For 246 years, Black people living in colonial America and later the United States were enslaved, and even those who were free were restricted and subjugated to subhuman status because of the beliefs Europeans held about them. These beliefs are the roots of what culminated in legislation and were ultimately responsible for the dehumanization and enslavement of Black people.

In closing, I did not go into details about the enslavement of Black people in the United States because I am not sure that is part of my story. Therefore, the research on my family history continues. I encourage you to do two things to deepen your perspective on the enslavement of Black people in America. First, read the book and watch the movie. *12 Years a Slave*. Second, read the speech given by Frederick Douglass, "What to the slave is the 4th of July?" which is the title of this chapter. He provides a detailed account of slavery while highlighting the truth about the capabilities and intelligence of Black Americans. Lastly, reading Douglass's speech will set the stage for Chapter 2, answering two questions: Who were Black people before and during enslavement? And does the history of Black people disprove the beliefs held in Europe, colonial America, and later the United States regarding their supposed racial inferiority to white people?

CHAPTER 2

"If you teach the Negro that he has accomplished as much good as any other race, he will aspire to equality and justice without regard to race."
~ Carter G. Woodson
The Mis-Education of the Negro

Overview of Black History: From Africa to the United States

From my work in public education for over 20 years and being an educational consultant across the country, I know that the history of Black people that is taught in schools begins with slavery and briefly touches on the modern Civil Rights Movement. There may be pockets of progressive work, but the story of Black Americans does not exist as it should in a K–12 setting. Limiting the history of Black people to a restricted focus on the historical period containing enslavement and colonization is historical discontinuity. It is a broken history. In this chapter, I will provide evidence to prove that Black people are not an inferior group of human beings, and I will do that by highlighting several African civilizations that predate European civilizations and the transatlantic slave trade. Furthermore, I will call attention to the contributions Black Americans made during the period of American slavery, as well as those who rebelled against the institution of slavery.

Thousands of years before the transatlantic slave trade, there were thriving African civilizations. The Kingdom of Benin, for instance, flourished from 1100 AD until 1897. This kingdom, located in what is now southwestern Nigeria, lasted for nearly 800 years and was a testament to the resilience and ingenuity of the Benin people. They were highly sophisticated in the arts and bronze working. During the 15th and 16th centuries, they traded with the Europeans and Portuguese, exchanging cloth, pepper, and ivory for guns, powder, metals, and salts.

The kingdom ended in 1897 when British troops invaded and sacked the capital, Benin, an extremely wealthy city in the kingdom, and looted it of all its wealth. In particular, they stole the Benin bronzes, fantastic artwork made by expert artisans in the 13th through 16th centuries. These Benin bronzes, known for their intricate designs and historical significance, are now in museums across Britain, and Benin's government is fighting to get them back. It has been a years-long fight, but they are now starting to get some of their artwork back so it can be placed in their museums.

The West African Kingdom of Mali arose in the early 13th century, and its first king was Sundiata Keita. If you have ever seen Disney's *The Lion King*, it is the story of Sundiata Keita. I am disappointed that Disney has not corrected this, but why does a movie about an African kingdom have to use animals? Yes, the lion is strong, but why are they using animals? Other Disney films about princes, princesses, kings, and queens do not use animals, so why do it with an African kingdom?

The Kingdom of Mali was a powerful country. Timbuktu and Djenne were Mali's most important cities. Religiously, it was an Islamic country, but that does not mean the people were not Black. The people of Mali built elaborate mosques and Islamic schools. The library at St. Cora University in Timbuktu held an estimated 700,000 manuscripts. The Kingdom of Mali ruled West Africa from 1280 until about 1600 AD and was a powerhouse. Mansa Musa, its most recognized ruler, was considered the wealthiest person ever, with an estimated net worth exceeding $400 billion. During his reign, Mali was the largest producer of gold in the world, a testament to the kingdom's wealth and power.

Following the decline of Mali, the West African empire of Songhai emerged during the 15th and 16th centuries after the Kingdom of Mali declined. Songhai embraced some of the areas formerly controlled by the Kingdom of Mali. The Songhai Empire was the largest and last of the three major pre-colonial empires in West Africa. At its peak, it was larger than Western Europe. Soon after the decline of Songhai, the transatlantic slave trade arose, driven not just by Europeans but also by Arabs.

On the continent's eastern side, the history of Black people dates back more than 8,000 years, beginning in Ethiopia. North of Ethiopia was the Nubian Empire, a civilization that dates back as far as 3,800 BCE and continues to exist today. The Nubians, an ancient people who currently live in Egypt and Sudan, are considered indigenous to Northern Africa. The Nubian Empire was mighty militarily and known for having master archers. Nubia was also a center of intellectual achievement, with a rich literature and language history. Modern Nubians, who still live in their ancestral homelands and continue to speak the Nubian language today, are a living testament to this legacy. The legacy of the Nubians includes historical evidence pointing to this region of Africa as the root of what would emerge as ancient Egypt.

North of Nubia is Egypt. Egypt is recognized as one of the first civilizations in human history and is the most studied. Egyptology, the study of Egypt, is the only academic study solely committed to studying an ancient civilization. It can be argued that Egyptology was established to erase the Black origins of this great ancient civilization. American sociologist WEB DuBois argues Egyptology was a form of scientific racism, which flourished in the 19th century. DuBois published *The World and Africa*, and in it, he writes, "There can be but one explanation for this vagary of nineteenth-century science. It was due to the slave trade and Negro slavery. It was due to the fact that the rise and support of capitalism called for the rationalization based upon degrading and discrediting the Negroid peoples. Significantly, the science of Egyptology arose and flourished at the very time that the cotton kingdom reached its greatest power on the foundation of American Negro slavery." There is further evidence that supports DuBois's argument about Egyptology.

Constantine de Volney, a Frenchman, journeyed through Egypt from 1783 to 1785. He published a best-selling book in France about his travels to Egypt called *The Ruins of Empires*. The book was in high demand in Britain and the United States. However, because of racism in the United States, the British editors removed the following passage from Volney's book: "There are a people, now forgotten, who discovered, while others were yet barbarians, the elements of arts and sciences. A race of men, now ejected from society for their sable skin and frizzled hair, founded on the study of the laws of nature, those civil and religious systems which still govern the universe."

Volney describes the indigenous people of ancient Egypt as

Black or African. Other historical figures, such as Herodotus, Homer, and Aristotle from ancient Greece, have described the builders of the Egyptian civilization as Ethiopian or "Black-skinned" and having "wooly hair." There is also an expansive list of Black scholars who have written about ancient Egypt and its Black African roots. W.E.B. DuBois, Carter G. Woodson, Cheikh Anta Diop, Ivan Van Sertima, John Henrik Clarke, Anthony West, Asa Hilliard, and Tony Browder are some of the Black scholars that I have read on my lifelong journey of "knowledge of self." However, in most curricula in the United States of America and even in Egypt today, ancient Europeans or people from the Mediterranean are credited with building ancient Egypt.

During the summer of 2013, I went on a two-week study tour of ancient Egypt with Tony Browder and approximately 120 other African Americans. This pilgrimage has been coined by participants of Browder's trip as a "Kemetamorphosis." Kemetamorphosis means looking at ancient Egypt from its origins, focusing on the Black African indigenous population who gave birth to that civilization, and embracing this history as part of our ancestral lineage. Egypt's original name, Kemet, which means "the black land," dates back more than six millennia. Ancient Egyptian civilization is divided into periods. Pre-dynastic Egypt dates back at least 5,000 years, followed by the first dynastic period of the Old Kingdom, which began in 3,160 BCE and lasted over 1,000 years. Ancient Egypt lasted almost 2,000 years, free of foreign invasion. In 1783 BCE, the Hyksos invaded Egypt and ended the 300 years known as the Middle Kingdom.

It was not until the Assyrians conquered Egypt in 664 BCE that Egypt began a period in which it would undergo rulership by many outside invaders, including Greece and Rome, and the last conquest of Egypt happened in 651 AD by the Arabs. In the United States, several movies, such as *The Ten Commandments, Cleopatra,* and *Gods of Egypt,* portray ancient Egyptians as white. Children's books and social studies textbooks perpetuate the same image of Ancient Egyptians as being European or from the Mediterranean. Contrary to Hollywood and most books, historical evidence and DNA testing prove the indigenous people of ancient Egypt were Black.

While in Egypt, I visited the Giza pyramids, cruised the Nile River, and visited the great temples of Waset, Saqqara, Luxor, Dendara, Abydos, Amenhotep III, Hatshepsut, Karnak, Kham Ambo, Abu Simbel, and the Valley of the Kings.

My eyes did not lie. The depictions of the people everywhere I visited looked like me and not like Europeans. I know now, without a doubt, that the progenitors of ancient Egypt were Black Africans. From ancient Egypt to Mali, Black Africans built civilizations for over 7,000 years before Europe became civilized. The rich history of Black Africans did not stop when we arrived in America. Whether free or enslaved, Black people continued to dispel the ideology of Black racial inferiority under the most inhumane conditions imagined. I will highlight some of the people who contributed to the building of this nation.

First is John Baptiste Pointe du Sable, born in San Domingo, Haiti. He was a frontier trader, trapper, farmer, entrepreneur, peacekeeper, and protector of Native Americans. He was well known for trading goods throughout the Midwest, and he expanded his cabin to a trading post, which later became a small community with a church, school, and store. He founded a settlement that later became the city of Chicago in 1779. He was a successful Black man who eventually owned commercial buildings and docks and had a mansion with fruit orchards and livestock.

Benjamin Banneker, who lived from 1731 to 1806, was a free, self-taught mathematician, astronomer, and author of the first almanac in the United States, along with other publications. At 15, he took over his family farm and created an irrigation system to control water flow to the crops. Banneker is responsible for inventing the first clock in America in the 1750s. He was one of the primary surveyors for the territory and the construction of what we know today as Washington, D.C. He also corresponded with Thomas Jefferson on slavery and racial equality.

Jupiter Hammon, who lived from 1711 to 1806, was born into slavery in New York, as slavery was legal everywhere. He was enslaved by the Lloyd family of Queens on Long Island, New York. Unlike most enslaved people, his father had learned how to read and write. The Lloyd family encouraged Jupiter to attend school whenever he could, and he did. Jupiter served as a domestic servant, clerk, farmhand, and artisan. In 1760, he became the first Black to have a poem published in the United States of America, "An Evening Thought: Salvation by Christ, with the Penitential Cries." One of the major lines from that poem is, "If we should ever get to heaven, we shall find nobody to reproach us for being Black or being slaves."

Phyllis Wheatley was born in West Africa and sold into slavery at the age of seven or eight. The Wheatley family of Boston purchased her, and they taught her how to read and write in 16 months. At a young age, she could read the Bible, Greek and Latin classics, and British literature. In 1773, she published her first works in England, "poems on various subjects, religious and moral." Her work was criticized and had to be authenticated by John Hancock.

Sojourner Truth lived from 1797 to 1883. She was born into slavery 95 miles north of New York City. She was sold four times, and she and her youngest daughter finally escaped to freedom in 1826. Once free, Truth looked for the rest of her family, went to court, and won the freedom of one of her sons, who had been returned to the South. This made her one of the first Black women to challenge a white man in a United States court successfully. Sojourner was an abolitionist and recruited Black soldiers for the Union Army. She also advocated for prison reform, property rights, and universal suffrage.

Elijah McCoy, who lived from 1844 to 1929, was the son of former enslaved parents who escaped via the Underground Railroad to Canada. He was educated in Scotland and became a mechanical engineer. He is noted for having over 57 U.S. patents, mainly involved in the lubrication of steam engines. However, he could only sell his patents for a fraction of their worth. At the same time, his inventions made other white Americans millionaires.

Martin Delaney, who lived from 1812 to 1885, was an abolitionist, a journalist, a physician, a writer, and, arguably, the first proponent of Black nationalism. He was commissioned as a major and the first Black field officer in the U.S. Army and was one of three Black men to enroll in Harvard Medical College in 1850.

In the midst of slavery and second-class citizenship, Black Americans not only thrived and fought for equality but also demonstrated patriotism by serving the country militarily. Blacks participated in the Revolutionary and Civil Wars. During the Revolutionary War, both freed and enslaved Black men served bravely in the battles at Lexington, Concord, and Bunker Hill. At Bunker Hill, there were notable Blacks like Peter Salem, Barzilai Lou, Blaney Groucha, Titus Coburn, Alexander Ames, Cato Howe, Seymour Burr, and Salem Poor. White officers spoke about the Black soldiers' ability to be at the same level, if not better, than their white counterparts during the Revolutionary War.

When the war started, Blacks could not enlist in the Continental Army. On the contrary, the British issued the Dunmore Proclamation, which opened up the enlistment of Blacks in the

British Army. The Dunmore Proclamation guaranteed Black people freedom if they were to fight for the British and the British were to win the war. Initially, Washington did not want to do that. Still, he saw that Britain was gaining an advantage by enlisting Black soldiers while, at the same time, witnessing a reduction in his enlistment of military men because of desertion. It can be argued that Washington was forced to open up the door for Blacks to enlist. That gave the Continental Army the needed edge; eventually, the U.S. won the war, and the Blacks who fought for white America's independence remained enslaved or second-class citizens.

By the end of the war, the United States Army reported that Blacks accounted for about 10% to 15% of the soldiers in the Continental Army. The most notable Black regiment was the 1st Rhode Island. They were a thoroughly segregated unit run by white officers and are well known for their involvement in the Battle of Newport at Rhode Island. They fought so valiantly that the opposing officer resigned his commission rather than lead his men back into battle against them.

During the Civil War, Black Americans continued to believe in the promise of the United States and served bravely for the Union Army. It is estimated that more than 200,000 Blacks served in the Union Army during the Civil War. By July of 1865, 123,156 Blacks were enlisted in the Union Army. There were 120 infantry regiments with almost 100,000 Black men and 12 heavy artillery regiments with around 16,000 Black men. Ten light artillery regiments had close to 1,400 Black men, and seven cavalry regiments held about 7,300 Black men. In all, over 40,000 Black soldiers died during the Civil War, the majority of them from disease. Many Black soldiers were promoted to officers during the war, and 18 were awarded the Medal of Honor. The most recognized Union regiment during the Civil War was the 54th Massachusetts Regiment. In both wars, the reason why Washington and Lincoln needed Black troops was due to whites deserting the army.

While it is essential to note the contributions and the participation of Black Americans in the Revolutionary and Civil Wars, it is equally important to acknowledge that the horrors of being enslaved pushed Black Americans to the brink of running away from the plantation in which they were enslaved and actual rebellion. Most Americans are familiar with the Underground Railroad and the role Harriet Tubman played in helping more than 300 enslaved Blacks find freedom in the North. However, the Underground Railroad was much more expansive and had routes to freedom that went south into Florida and Mexico. At times, running away from slavery and engaging in rebellion were intertwined in the Black American story.

For example, the Seminole Indians in Florida have a history of conflict with the United States. There were enslaved Blacks who ran away from slavery in the Carolinas to Florida because Florida, at the time, was controlled by the Spanish. A Native American tribe of Creek origin helped Blacks who fled from the Carolinas and embraced them into their communities. They would become known as the Seminoles, a mixed tribe of the Native Creeks and Black Americans, who settled in Florida's northwest and central areas. However, as the U.S. began to occupy Florida, the Seminoles went to war with them.

There were two Seminole wars. The first lasted from 1817 to 1818. Andrew Jackson led the U.S. troops during the first war and succeeded. Shortly after, Spain signed a treaty that gave the United States Florida. The Second Seminole War lasted from 1835 to 1842. The Seminoles lost both wars and were forced to relocate west and became the victims of the Native American Trail of Tears.

One notable Black Seminole leader, John Horse, helped in the Second Seminole War and led the most extensive mass slave escape in U.S. history from Florida to Oklahoma and eventually Mexico. John Horse founded free Black settlements in Oklahoma and Mexico. While in Mexico, he secured the communal title for the Black Seminoles to their land grant, where their descendants still live today.

The Seminole Wars were one form of resistance in which running away from slavery and engaging in rebellion were intertwined. However, I would be remiss not to talk about the Black folks who were wholly opposed to enslavement and believed insurrection was the only path to freedom.

There were several slave revolts that happened across the United States of America during the period of slavery, and all of them were unsuccessful. The only successful slave revolt in the Western Hemisphere was led by Toussaint Louverture, an enslaved carriage driver who galvanized enslaved Blacks, whites who were part of the indentured servitude class, and others who were part of the indigenous population to revolt against France. Known as the Haitian Revolution, Louverture went to war against France from 1791 to 1804. The enslaved Africans won their independence from France and were able to claim Haiti as an independent nation. Consequently, the Haitian Revolution and other military campaigns in Egypt were crushing the French economy. Being in multiple wars forced France to sell the Louisiana territory to the United States in 1804, which is known as the Louisiana Purchase. The Louisiana Purchase opened the door for the United States to expand westward to the Pacific Ocean. Despite the lack of success, in his writings, Henry Louis Gates, a scholar of Black History, highlights five major slave revolts that occurred in the United States.

The first was the Stono Rebellion, the largest slave revolt ever staged in the 13 colonies. In this revolt, 20 enslaved people, under the leadership of Jimmy, organized and raided a warehouse-like store called Hutchinson's. They executed the white owners of Hutchinson's and placed their heads on the store steps for all to see. They then tried to make their way to St. Augustine, Florida, where they could secure their freedom. They were unsuccessful, and the rebellion was crushed in a week. Over a hundred enslaved Black people participated in the insurrection.

The second revolt was the New York Conspiracy of 1741. In Fort George, New York, a series of fires erupted, destroying several buildings. A group of whites, including a 16-year-old Irish indentured servant under arrest for theft, claimed that they overheard enslaved people bragging about setting the fires and plotting to kill white men and seize white women. In the investigation that followed, 30 Black men, two white men, and two white women were executed. More than 70 Blacks were exiled to Newfoundland and Haiti. By the end of the summer of 1741, 17 more Blacks were hanged, and 13 more were burned at the stake.

The third revolt was Gabriel Prosser's Conspiracy of 1800. Gabriel Prosser was enslaved and owned by Thomas Prosser. Gabriel was a skilled blacksmith who could read and write and found inspiration in the French and Saint Domingue Revolutions and the Haitian revolution that Toussaint L'Ouverture led. Prosser believed that Jeffersonian democratic ideology encompassed the interests of enslaved Blacks and working whites. If united, these two groups could oppose the oppressive Federalist merchant class. His goal was to rally a thousand enslaved people under his banner of death or liberty and then march on Richmond, Virginia, take the armory, and hold Governor James Monroe hostage. His plan was well advertised, but there was a severe thunderstorm on the day of the attack, and many of his followers lost faith. Prosser proceeded with the plan but was captured with 25 others because he was betrayed by an enslaved person named Pharaoh. All 25 insurrectionists, including Gabriel, were sent to the gallows and executed.

The fourth slave revolt was the German Coast uprising of 1811, led by Charles Deslondes, a mulatto enslaved driver who was also inspired by the Haitian Revolution. Author Daniel Rasmussen, a white Harvard-educated investigative journalist, identified this uprising as the most sophisticated slave revolt in United States history in his book, *American Uprising: The Untold Story of America's Largest Slave Revolt*. Deslondes, alongside 25 other enslaved Blacks, attacked the Andry plantation outside of New Orleans. They killed the plantation owner's family, and the owner escaped. As they marched towards New Orleans to seize the city, it was estimated that nearly three hundred enslaved Blacks had joined the rebellion. South Carolina Congressman Wade Hampton was charged with leading the suppression of the slave revolt, and he succeeded after two days when the enslaved Blacks ran out of ammunition. Most of the insurrectionists were killed during the battle. Some became prisoners, and others fled into the swamps.

Arguably the most famous revolt of all was Nat Turner's Rebellion of 1831. As a child, Nat Turner impressed his family and friends with his unusual sense of purpose. Driven by a prophetic vision and joined by a host of followers, Turner and 70 armed enslaved Black people, along with some free Blacks, set off to slaughter the white neighbors who had enslaved them. Turner and the insurrectionists attacked 15 homes and killed between 55 and 60 whites as they marched toward Jerusalem, Virginia. Other enslaved people who had planned to join Turner retreated after white militia groups began to attack Turner's men. Turner was able to elude the authorities for over a month before he was seized by a white man who stumbled upon his hideout. Most of the insurrectionists were caught and eventually killed or hanged.

In 2016, the story of Nat Turner became a motion film directed by Nate Parker, a Black American actor. The United States eventually went to war with itself for four years over the issue of slavery. Known as the United States Civil War, the endgame of the war resulted in the abolishment of slavery.

People of African descent have a rich history that rivals those worldwide, and it deserves its rightful place in world history and United States history. The history of Africa and its people has played a significant role in building this nation and making it the greatest nation on earth. Black Americans with family histories in America predating the Civil War have a story, unlike any other citizen. We are not part of the slogan, "We are a nation of immigrants," that this nation prides itself on. We are a product of forced immigration. We are part of a society that created a lie about the humanity of Black people. This lie is still pervasive in the minds of most Americans, including Black youth. The only way to combat this lie of racial inferiority is through truth. The quote at the beginning of this chapter by Carter G. Woodson emphasizes the importance of acknowledging the historical achievements of Black people. It underlies the idea that a comprehensive understanding of Black history can inspire a sense of equality and justice, irrespective of race.

CHAPTER 3

The problem of the 20th century is the problem of the color line.
~ W.E.B. DuBois
Souls of Black Folk
Overview of Black America: 1865-1954

With the end of the Civil War, the nation entered the Reconstruction Era from 1865-1877. During this period, the federal government ratified the Constitution's 13th, 14th, and 15th Amendments to support the newly freed Blacks in the United States. The 13th Amendment ended chattel slavery. The 14th Amendment guaranteed Black Americans citizenship, equal protection under the law and due process of law. And the 15th Amendment granted Black American men the right to vote. The federal government also passed "An Act to Establish a Bureau for the Relief of Freedmen and Refugees," establishing the Freedmen's Bureau. During Reconstruction, opportunities for Black

Americans to develop themselves were available. For the first time, Black Americans could integrate into the mainstream United States culture through education, employment, and politics.

The Freedmen's Bureau, which supported newly freed Blacks socially, politically, economically, and educationally, built over a thousand schools for freedmen in 1870 and established the first public schools for Black and white children in the South. The Bureau also employed Blacks and whites in the South during Reconstruction. The Freedmen's Bureau employed my great-great-great-grandfather, Taylor Holden, from 1865 until 1877.

Politically, more than two thousand Black Americans held public office from the local level to the U.S. Senate. About half of all Black Americans who served in Congress during this period were from South Carolina and Louisiana. In Mississippi, where my family would later reside, Hiram Revels became the first Black American elected to the U.S. Senate. He replaced the vacant seat of Jefferson Davis but did not serve a full term. Following Revels was Blanche Kelso Bruce, who was elected to the U.S. Senate from Mississippi and served from 1875 until 1881, the first African American to serve a full term. Mississippi has not elected another Black person to the United States Senate despite Mississippi having the highest percentage of Blacks in the nation.

Despite gains made by Black Americans during Reconstruction, the 13th, 14th, and 15th Amendments were disregarded by Southern states through the creation of Black Codes. Black Codes were laws passed by Southern states in 1865 that were modified versions of slave codes, laws that restricted Black Americans' freedom. Mississippi was the first state to pass Black Codes, and it didn't take long for the rest of the South to establish a new system of racial discrimination and oppression. Over the next 30 years, a presidential election and Supreme Court case supported the institutionalization of Black codes and legalized this new system, known as Jim Crow.

Reconstruction came to an abrupt end with the presidential election of 1876. Known as the Compromise of 1877, Rutherford Hayes and Governor Tilden of New York were in a tightly contested presidential election. Neither candidate would concede the election. In exchange for the presidency, Rutherford Hayes, the Republican candidate, agreed to end Reconstruction. As a result of the compromise, all U.S. troops and the workers of the Freedmen's Bureau were removed from the South, and Southern states were provided legislative support from the federal government to help industrialize and rebuild the South's economy.

Nearly two decades later, in 1896, the United States Supreme Court handed down the Plessy v. Ferguson decision. This case originated when Homer Plessy, in Louisiana, challenged the Separate Car Act, which required railroads to have separate cars for Blacks and whites. In a way, Plessy was the first Rosa Parks because he sat in a whites-only car and refused to move. He was arrested, charged, and convicted. Using the court appeals process, the case went to the United States Supreme Court, which upheld the constitutionality of racial segregation under the separate but equal doctrine.

It was an eight-to-one ruling, with only Justice Harlan dissenting. In his dissent, he wrote, "The white race deems itself to be the dominant race in this country. Thus, it is in prestige and achievements in education and wealth and in power. But in the view of the Constitution, in the eye of the law, there is no superior, dominant ruling class of citizens." The "separate but equal" doctrine led to the proliferation of segregation in the North and the South. In the South, segregation was de jure, or by law, while in the North, it was de facto, meaning voluntarily. Though not enforced by law, as you will see in later chapters, de facto segregation created racial discrimination and inequality the same way de jure did. In reality, the Plessy decision created separate and unequal conditions.

For example, three years after Plessy v. Ferguson, the Supreme Court heard another case that would perpetuate racial discrimination against Black Americans leading into the 20th century. In Cumming v. Richmond, the Supreme Court ruled in favor of allowing states to levy taxes on Black and white citizens alike while providing public schools for white children only. In other words, Black homeowners were paying property taxes to local municipalities even though they were not required to build schools for or educate Black children.

At the turn of the century, the United States entered the Progressive Era, a time of business expansion, urbanization, and immigration. Moreover, the intellectual elites of the United States during this era began to build on the work of Charles Darwin's theory of natural selection, or "survival of the fittest." Darwin's cousin, Sir Francis Galton, coined the term "eugenics," which is "the study of how to arrange reproduction within a human population to increase the occurrences of heritable characteristics as desirable."

White intellectual elites and scholars of eugenics in the United States during the early 20th century believed that the Nordics, Scots, Germans, and people from other European stock from North and West Europe were the dominant race within the human family. Blacks continued to be placed at the lowest point of human existence, while Eastern and Southern Europeans were also seen as inferior to the Europeans from the North and West. In many ways, the rise of eugenics was the manifestation of the beliefs and prior work of European scholars of natural history or the laws of nature into the 20th-century belief system and way of life in the United States.

The following are passages from the writings of white intellectual elites from the Progressive Era who perpetuated the belief that whites were superior to Blacks.

American journalist and essayist H.L. Mencken: "It is apparent, on brief reflection, that the Negro, no matter how much he is educated, must remain, as a race, in a condition of subservience; that he must remain the inferior of the stronger and more intelligent white man so long as he retains racial differentiation."

American lawyer, zoologist and anthropologist Madison Grant: "The intelligence and ability of a colored person are in pretty direct proportion to the amount of white blood he has, and that most of the positions of leadership, influence, and prominence in the Negro race are held not by real Negroes but by Mulattoes, many of whom have very little Negro blood. This is so true that to find a Black Negro in a conspicuous position is a matter of comment."

Famous author Jack London (considered a progressive proponent of eugenics) had this to say about Black people: "The Negro races, the mongrel races, the slavish races, the unprogressive races, are of bad blood—that is, of blood which is not qualified to permit them to successfully survive the selection by which the fittest survive." White intellectual elites were not the only ones who held these beliefs. President Woodrow Wilson, who served two terms from 1913–1921, had the same mindset.

President Wilson, who was politically astute, corresponded with Black scholar W.E.B. DuBois, and Wilson convinced DuBois to endorse him for the presidency. Wilson ended up disappointing DuBois because of the decisions that Wilson's administration made. According to Arthur Link, Wilson's biographer, cabinet members Albert Burleson and William Gibbs McAdoo removed all Black political appointees in the South and allowed local postmasters to downgrade Black workers with civil service status.

Furthermore, President Wilson held a private showing of *The Birth of a Nation*, a movie based on the book *The Clansman*. The movie portrays Black Americans as criminals while hailing the Ku Klux Klan as the saviors and heroes of the Black villain. Wilson said that this film, now widely considered to be one of the most racist in history, "is like writing with lightning. And my only regret is that it is all so terribly true."

The portrayal of Black Americans as criminals on the big screen played out in real life for hundreds of thousands of Blacks who fell victim to convict leasing. While the 13th Amendment ended chattel slavery, it did not end slavery in the United States. The 13th Amendment reads, "Neither slavery nor involuntary servitude, except as a punishment for a crime, whereof the party shall have been duly convicted, shall exist within the United States or any place subject to their jurisdiction." The 13th Amendment ended chattel slavery, yet slavery remained legal as a means of punishment for crime.

From the end of Reconstruction through the 1950s, hundreds of thousands of Blacks were convicted for violating vagrancy laws. Vagrancy considered acts such as loitering or being unemployed as a crime. Blacks who were convicted of vagrancy crimes received harsh sentences. Considered misdemeanors today, Blacks would receive convictions and years in prison for these crimes. These laws were a way to get around the 13th Amendment and put formerly enslaved Black Americans back to work in a new form of slavery called convict leasing. Convict leasing was a system of penal labor practiced in the Southern United States after Reconstruction. It provided prison labor to private parties such as former plantation owners and corporations. The Tennessee Coal, Iron, and Railroad, one of the 12 original companies from the Dow Jones Industrial Index, and U.S. Steel, the world's largest company at the time, were major users of this prison labor. In the 1870s,

95% of America's prison system was Black, and by 1898, 73% of Alabama's annual state revenue came from convict leasing.

While the antebellum form of slavery ended in 1865 with the ratification of the 13th Amendment, it opened up the door for Black Americans to now become state property. Big corporations and former plantation owners who formerly enslaved people were able to purchase labor from the prison system at an extremely cheap cost. In many ways, convict leasing created working conditions for Blacks that were more harsh than being enslaved. This new reality for Black Americans, being leased for labor, also exposed Black Americans to brutal beatings that at times led to death. If the prisoner was killed, corporations or former plantation owners had to pay a small fine, were free of criminal charges, and were allowed to lease more convicts for labor. This period was one of terror for Black Americans.

Frederick Douglass opposed this new system of oppression and said, "The convict lease system and lynch law are twin infamies which flourished hand in hand in many of the United States. They are the two great outgrowths and results of the class legislation under which our people suffer." Douglass also mentions lynch laws, which were an acknowledgment of horrific violence being inflicted on Black Americans by white Americans. According to the Equal Justice Initiative, there were well over four thousand documented lynchings between 1877 and 1950. Mississippi had the most out of ten Southern states, with 654, and Bolivar County, where my family was living during this time period, was eighth amongst counties in Mississippi with the highest number of lynchings.

For decades, Black Americans experienced violence equal to modern-day horror movies. Across the nation, lynchings of Black Americans served as a form of entertainment for white Americans. The lynchings of Black Americans were advertised in newspapers and some white churches and were often held on Sunday afternoons. At times, lynchings would have thousands of white Americans participating, including children. Photographs of these gruesome acts were made and sold as postcards. I have a close friend and colleague whose great cousin was lynched upon returning to the United States after serving in World War I. His name is Clinton Briggs. In 1919, after coming home from the war, Clinton Briggs was living in Arkansas, and one day, while walking down the sidewalk, he refused to step aside for a white woman who was coming in the opposite direction. When the white woman said something to him, he politely replied, "Ma'am, this is a free country." She reported that to local law enforcement, and he was arrested. Later that night, he was lynched by a mob of white people.

The violence escalated beyond just lynchings. During the summer of 1919, also known as the Red Summer, white Americans felt resentment at the end of World War I. With well over a million soldiers coming back, including Black soldiers, there was stiff competition for jobs. This created tension between Black and white communities, and as a result, over 25 race riots broke out across the United States of America. Most Black Americans were law-abiding citizens, minded their own business, and established thriving communities within Jim Crow. Hatred of Black people was so embedded in the psyche of white America that false accusations would incite white violence. There are several accounts of entire Black communities being nearly destroyed during the 20th century, with one of the most recognized being Rosewood. In the '90s, Black movie filmmaker John Singleton released Rosewood, a true story about a Black town in Florida being destroyed by local white residents because a white woman lied about being raped by a Black man despite people knowing she was having an extramarital affair with another white man.

Another notable Black community that was destroyed in 1921 was Black Wall Street, a racially segregated Black community in Tulsa, Oklahoma. Because of the oil boom in Oklahoma, jobs were plentiful, even for Blacks living in the area. The Black side of Tulsa, aka Black Wall Street, developed its own social, political, educational, and economic infrastructures. In many ways, it outmatched Tulsa's white side.

Nevertheless, an event occurred between a Black male teenager and a white woman in an elevator that was exaggerated. What resulted was a massacre that lasted 24 hours. The white violence inflicted on Black Wall Street resulted in 191 businesses being destroyed, including churches, schools, and a hospital. 1,256 homes were destroyed, with more than 300 Black people being killed and 714 wounded.

Despite the 13th, 14th, and 15th Amendments granting the same rights to Black Americans as white Americans, they were violated and backed by violence. Social and political disenfranchisement ruled the day for Black Americans during the first half of the 20th century. Furthermore, overt economic discrimination towards Black Americans in the federal government occurred during the late 19th through mid-20th centuries.

For example, the Homestead Act was a government assistance program to help citizens develop, cultivate, and own farmland nationwide. The Act declared that any adult or intended citizen who had never borne arms against the United States government could claim up to 160 acres of surveyed government land. They were required to improve the plot by building a dwelling and cultivating the land. America at the time was an agrarian economy, so getting 160 acres of prime real estate was a tremendous opportunity for white Americans to establish wealth because it guaranteed ownership of the cultivated land after five years. The United States gave away more than 160 million acres of public land to over 1.6 million homesteaders. The Homestead Act excluded Black people, benefited white Americans, and was another policy that exacerbated income inequality between Black and white Americans after the period of enslavement.

Nearly four decades later, in 1934, the Federal Housing Authority (FHA) was established during the Great Depression as part of the New Deal. The FHA insured home mortgages and made home ownership affordable while providing funding to increase employment in home construction. Black Americans were denied the right to participate in these programs, which established the middle class in the United States. Through redlining and restrictive covenants, Black Americans were restricted from purchasing homes in desirable neighborhoods with higher home values. Three years later, the Housing Act of 1937 was passed by Congress. The Act provided subsidies for local public housing agencies to improve living conditions for low-income families. The policies from the FHA exacerbated racial segregation, placing Blacks in the housing projects while white Americans had access to homeownership in newly developed neighborhoods with higher property values. The American dream is to own a home and, through homeownership, establish generational wealth. The Homestead Act and New Deal policies, which would be considered welfare programs in today's society, helped whites own land and homes while building generational wealth but excluded Blacks. Even Black Americans who served their country in the military were denied access to the G.I. Bill, which was a program established in the 1940s to assist military veterans.

For Black Americans, the first half of the 20th century was full of oppression, discrimination, and violence. However, when opportunity did present itself, Black America thrived and contributed to the betterment of the United States. For example, Black Wall Street and Rosewood were not the only thriving Black communities in the 20th century. Communities such as Wilmington, North Carolina; Bronzeville on the South Side of Chicago; and Harlem, New York, with the Harlem Renaissance, thrived despite the pervasive inequality across the United States. Educationally, Black Americans benefited from the establishment of Historically Black Colleges and Universities (HBCUs).

In 1890, the federal government granted land to Black colleges and universities.19 institutions were established with a focus on agriculture, mechanical, and industrial education. Alcorn State University in Lorman, Mississippi, was one of the 19 Black colleges established by the federal government, and that is where my grandfather received his college education. In the early 20th century, predominantly Black fraternities and sororities established themselves in predominantly white and predominantly Black universities to continue to fight for civil rights. Omega Psi Phi Fraternity was the first Black fraternity founded on a Black college campus on November 17, 1911. I am referencing the Omega Psi Phi because my father, uncle, and I are members.

Black intellects who studied at Harvard, such as W.E.B. Du Bois and Carter G. Woodson, pushed for the education and empowerment of Black Americans during the first half of the 20th century. Carter G. Woodson, the father of Black History in the United States, established Negro History Week in 1926. Lastly, several Black American inventors significantly contributed to advancing the nation and humanity. Alice Parker invented and patented the first central heating furnace system. Garrett Morgan invented the gas mask and the three-way stoplight. George Washington Carver discovered over 300 new uses for the peanut and improved crop rotation, the practice of planting crops to maintain strong soil health. Moreover, Frederick McKinley Jones invented the refrigerated truck. Consider the impact Benjamin Banneker, author of the first almanac in America, George Washington Carver's crop rotation innovation, and Frederick McKinley Jones's invention of the refrigerated truck had on the revolution and prosperity of the United States agrarian economy. These are a few examples and not an exhaustive list of what Black Americans have done to make the United States a great nation.

In closing this chapter, I want to share what I have learned about my family history during this time period. My great-grandparents, Morgan Brown and Eliza Holden, were married in the late 1880s in Mississippi. Mississippi was the first state to establish the Black Codes at the end of the Civil War in 1865. In 1890, further restrictions were placed on Black Mississippians when the Mississippi State Constitution was enacted. It strengthened existing Black Codes and codified into law separate schools for Blacks and whites.

After Reconstruction, all public education suffered under the new government in Mississippi, but Black schools were especially hard hit. For example, in the violence accompanying the Mississippi elections of 1875, which ended Republican rule in the state, several Black schools were burned, and both white and Black teachers of Black students were beaten or run out of town by white Mississippians.

The white backlash did not totally decimate schools, but by the 1940s, racial discrimination in teacher pay and per-pupil spending was pervasive. In 1940, the state of Mississippi was spending $41.71 per white student and $7.24 per Black student. Black teachers earned 30% of white teachers' pay. Most Black schools were wooden shacks, often without indoor plumbing, and the school year only lasted about six months so that Black students could have more time to be in the cotton fields during the planting and harvesting seasons. Luther Munford, in his book *Black Gravity: Desegregation in 30 Mississippi Districts*, states that Mississippi spent up to ten times as much per child on white education as it did on Negro education throughout the first half of the 20th century. As late as 1946, 16 counties had no Negro high schools, and only a tenth of the state's school-aged Black children were enrolled in school.

My grandfather overcame these barriers and earned a bachelor's degree from Alcorn State University in Lorman, Mississippi. He became a schoolteacher and taught for several decades. By 1940, my grandfather was teaching in Rosedale, Mississippi, and was married to my grandmother, Willie Mae. They owned their home, which was valued at one thousand dollars. According to the 1940 Census Bureau, my grandparents had taken in other less fortunate people.

Moreover, the 1940 United States Census also showed my grandfather earned $425 a year as a teacher, while white teachers, on average, were earning over $1400 a year. My grandfather was making less money with a college degree than white teachers, who had 3.5 years of college on average in Mississippi. When compounded annually, this created extreme income inequality for my grandparents, which ultimately negatively impacted their ability to build generational wealth. Discrimination at the ballot box was no different. Jim Crow laws in Mississippi prevented my grandfather from voting for the first time until he was 66 years old. His first vote in an election resulted from the Voting Rights Act of 1965.

My family played it right and did everything they could to be good, law-abiding citizens. Simply because of their melanated skin, they were discriminated against socially, politically, and economically. They were also living in a climate of intimidation, hatred, and violence. Despite extreme odds and the possibility of death, the Brown family leveraged their faith, love, and education and immersed themselves in the Civil Rights Movement.

CHAPTER 4

"I question America. Is this America the land of the free... where we have to sleep with our telephones off of the hooks... because we want to live as decent human beings, in America?
~ Fannie Lou Hamer
Testimony at the 1964 Democratic National Convention
Overview of Black America: 1954-1968

The Black American fight for civil rights does not begin with Dr. King but dates back to the founding of this nation. Several prominent Black activists predated Dr. King. Activists such as Benjamin Banneker corresponded with Thomas Jefferson on ending slavery. Alongside Banneker were David Walker, Frederick Douglass, Sojourner Truth, Harriet Tubman, Marcus Garvey, and Elijah Muhammad. While this list is not exhaustive, when we think about the fight for civil rights in the 1950s and 60s, we cannot disconnect it from the history of those who paved the way for Black America's new leaders during the 1950s and 1960s.

The Civil Rights Era (1954–1968) was a tumultuous time filled with progress and violence. The era began with a monumental Supreme Court decision, and through a series of strategic acts of civil disobedience, such as economic boycotts, rallies, marches, sit-ins, and other forms of political protest, civil rights activists applied pressure on the federal government to end discriminatory practices in systems across the nation. In 1954, the Supreme Court in the Brown v. Board of Education decision overturned the Plessy decision and ruled that racial segregation of schools was unconstitutional. In the 1960s, Congress passed the Civil Rights Act of 1964, which prohibited discrimination in public places; the Voting Rights Act of 1965, which ensured the vote of African Americans; and the Fair Housing Act of 1968, which prohibited discrimination in housing. Considered the Second Reconstruction, the civil rights bills of the 1960s primarily dealt with social and political discrimination. While these efforts were promising, in the words of Dr. King, "It didn't cost the government a dime." Nor did the civil rights bills of the 1960s deal with righting the wrong of decades of economic discrimination. While economic discrimination was generational, dating back to enslavement, Black Americans in 1954 still wielded significant economic spending power.

In 1954, the U.S. Department of Commerce and Johnson Publication, the African American-owned news company that published *Jet* and *Ebony* magazines, released a documentary highlighting the economic strength of Black America while trying to address the racist ideology that existed in the business sector across America.

The documentary, *The Secret of Selling the Negro*, attempted to convince white American business owners to open up their doors to Black consumers. The reason for this is that the producers of the film recognized the economic power of Black America. In 1954, Black Americans possessed 15 billion dollars of annual spending power. If Black America had been its own nation, it would have been one of the top ten wealthiest countries in the world. Black income reached record highs that year, and 33% of Black Americans were homeowners. Between 1930 and 1954, college enrollment of Blacks increased by 2,500%. The marriage rate in Black America was 65%, and Black homeowners paid their mortgages on time at a higher rate than white Americans. Despite everything that Blacks were up against, they worked hard and valued education and family.

The economic strength and ingenuity of the Black community were on full display in Montgomery, Alabama, when the Montgomery Improvement Association launched the Montgomery Bus Boycott, a highly organized economic boycott that lasted longer than a year. Despite efforts to disrupt and end the boycott, Black residents of Montgomery under the leadership of Dr. King persevered, did not ride buses, and won a major victory leading to the end of Jim Crow in Alabama. The Montgomery Bus Boycott is acknowledged as the birth of the modern Civil Rights Movement.

While the movement under the leadership of the Southern Christian Leadership Conference (SCLC) and Dr. King was nonviolent in its approach to fighting for equality, the violence inflicted on the Black community by white Americans did not stop. Every day, hard-working Black Americans, particularly in the South, experienced intimidation, violence, and death at the hands of white Americans in the 1960s. Violence was so widespread in the South, particularly in Alabama and Mississippi, that Black children were routinely being killed.

It was the murder of Emmett Till in 1955 that brought white violence inflicted on Black America to the national and global conscience. Emmett Till was a 13-year-old Black boy from Chicago, Illinois, who went to Mississippi to visit family for the summer, like I did in the '80s as a child. Emmett went to a store in Money, Mississippi, with his cousins and may have whistled or flirted with the store clerk, Carolyn Bryant, a white woman. Carolyn's husband and his half-brother found Emmett Till, kidnapped him, and brutally murdered him. His mother, Mamie Till, decided to have an open-casket funeral because she wanted the whole world to see what had happened to her son. Carolyn Bryant would later admit she lied about Emmett Till flirting with her.

On September 15, 1963, in Birmingham, Alabama, not even a month after the March on Washington, where King delivered his famous "I Have a Dream" speech, the 16th Street Baptist Church was bombed, killing four Black children: Addie Mae Collins, Denise McNair, Carol Robertson, and Cynthia Wesley. A few months prior to the bombing of the 16th Street Baptist Church, the Gaston Motel, where Dr. King spent most of his time when he was doing work in Birmingham, Alabama, was destroyed by a bomb

In the state of Mississippi in 1963 and 1964, respectively, Jackson, Mississippi, civil rights organizer Medgar Evers was gunned down and murdered in front of his home, and three civil rights workers, James Chaney, Andrew Goodman, and Michael Schwerner, were murdered in Mississippi by the Ku Klux Klan. Goodman and Schwerner were Jewish students who participated in Freedom Summer 1964. Moreover, in 1964, Fannie Lou Hamer, a civil rights activist from the Mississippi Delta, delivered a powerful testimony at the Democratic National Convention (DNC). She shared her story of trying to become a first-class citizen in Mississippi by registering to vote.

The consequences of such an act were steep. Hamer shared with the committee that she was a sharecropper. When the plantation owner found out she tried to register to vote, he threatened to terminate her from her job. This was not the worst of the consequences for Hamer's actions. Hamer also shared that she and others were arrested and jailed after attempting to register to vote. While jailed, Hamer described the horrendous way she and others were beaten. She closes her testimony in a powerful way by saying, "I question America. Is this America the land of the free... where we have to sleep with our telephones off of the hooks... because we want to live as decent human beings in America?"

Fannie Lou Hamer is from Ruleville, Mississippi, only 30 miles from Rosedale, Mississippi, my family's hometown. When Fannie Lou Hamer delivered her testimony at the DNC, my grandparents, father, and his siblings were actively involved in the movement with Hamer in the Mississippi Delta. Dr. King was such an iconic leader of the Civil Rights Movement that oftentimes, the activists who were on the ground leading rallies, marches, sit-ins, and other efforts are often forgotten. I am blessed to have a father and uncle who were willing to share their story of growing up in the Mississippi Delta and being part of the Civil Rights Movement there and later in Madison, Wisconsin.

For several years, I had them speak to teachers and students about their experiences in the Civil Rights Movement. Unfortunately, they shared with me how each time they tell their story, they are reliving the trauma from that time in their lives. Their story is powerful and has impacted thousands of educators and young people. And that is why I am dedicating this chapter to my father and my uncle. Following is a two-hour interview with my father and my uncle, unscripted and with slight edits, about their lived experience in Mississippi and how the Brown family values of faith, love, and education were powerful tools in overcoming the challenges of hate and violence.

PERCY BROWN, JR.

FAMILY INTERVIEW
Family Beliefs and Values Growing Up in the Mississippi Delta

Percy Jr. (Author):

What do you remember about Granddaddy and Grandmother in terms of who they were as parents to the two of you and your four other siblings? What are some of those fond memories that you have of your parents?

Charles:

Oh, man. I want to start with Mother. Mother, you know how women say they are standing by their husbands, but that was mother. Mother stood behind daddy 100% in terms of support.

My mother was a giant. It took me years to really think about how hard her job was. She was feeding a family of eight, and she worked in and outside of the home. She prepared great meals, but was a very, very, very strong woman who supported her family, supported her husband, and everything that he pursued.

Dad, Daddy, the educator. Daddy, I guess nowadays, and it took me many, many years to realize that I think both of our parents were progressive as we understand that term now. But Dad was a great educator. He instilled a lot of things in us, like the importance of family and valuing education. He protected us. I think we lived a pretty structured life because of that. He had absolutely high expectations of us in terms of how we performed in school. He was a patriarch and a disciplinarian. Would you agree, Percy, Sr. when he needed to be? Dad was the greatest father—besides your father, of course. Dad is the best dad ever.

Percy Jr.:

So, Uncle Charles, when you say Granddaddy was progressive, what do you mean by that, for that time period?

Charles:

Well, doing things that some people may have been afraid to do, for example, participating in the civil rights movement, putting his own life in harm's way, as well as his family. To take risks back then that would ordinarily be perhaps dangerous, or people didn't accept them.

And I think some more of that is going to come out through this interview where Percy, Sr. and I will share vivid examples of his progressiveness as a leader and a father and in the community. Even as an educator, he was very progressive.

Percy Sr.:

Yeah, I want to begin by just saying that what I remember first and foremost is we were blessed to have loving parents who definitely demonstrated love. We always talked of how this family was built on a foundation of love. And it was so strong that even all of the grandkids, the second generation, when they would come down south, Percy Jr., you and Latise, and all of Charles's kids, would experience that love, that strong love in our family. The second thing I would like to point out is that my parents were godly parents. They didn't just, like the old saying, go talk the talk, but they walked the walk. They lived a godly life in front of us and made sure that we went to Sunday school and church. We grew up in Sunday school and church, and we were very active in church.

Daddy was the head deacon of the church, and Mother was on the mother's board. She was a godly woman. That faith carried us on throughout our journey, even when we came to Wisconsin, and I ended up being the head deacon of the church that I belong to here. But it all started with my home life growing up and the modeling that came from our parents..

The third thing that really stands out is the sacrifice they made for us. They did a lot for us. I remember we used to chop and pick cotton ten hours a day. And even with that, Mother still got up early every morning and fixed a full breakfast. And she would go to the cotton fields right along with us, ten hours a day, come home, and have a full-course dinner prepared. And that was just one example of the sacrifice that they made for us. And I could go on and on and talk about that. The other thing I already mentioned and Charles mentioned is the example that they set. And I often tell people, I say, "My role model was my dad and mother; they were my role models."

And the last two things that jumped out at me are the counsel and the wisdom that Mother and Daddy shared. You could always feel comfortable going to them. Even when you messed up, you were still received. I remember my oldest brother; he was always in and out of jail, and Daddy would always say, "Well, this is the last time and he would go and get my brother out of jail." Daddy would be right up there, that forgiving kind of father.

Charles mentioned the discipline part, and I just want to add a footnote to the discipline part just to make sure everybody understood what is really meant. My dad was a schoolteacher, and back then, they paddled people. Daddy wore the paddle right on his waist in school. And Mother would use the switch a lot. So when we got out of line, we would get whippings. And I often call it today 'tough love,' but we did get those whippings where they were teaching us through strict discipline. And I do believe that that really paid off in the end.

Now, the last little thing about Mother in particular, she had a way that she could just read me and know if I was going through kind of a low point. I would not even necessarily say anything. And so she'd call me and say, "Hey, how are you doing?" I'd say, "I'm doing all right."

And she'd say, "Well, I just want to make sure you're OK." And somehow, she'd know that I was heavily burdened by something. And I always wondered, how would she know that, that instinct of just knowing that? And to this day, I think about that.

They just drilled into us the notion that you live by getting an education because they believed that the key to opportunity was to get a solid education. So, in our home, it wasn't an option about going to college, it was expected. We also had a hard work ethic that we developed working in the cotton fields. Furthermore, Daddy had a sideline construction company. We worked there too. But I'll tell you that education was the centerpiece of everything: our faith in God and our education.

The last piece is they always challenged us to look beyond ourselves and think of the bigger community and be considerate of the community by giving back to the community. And I always carry that with me as well as never forgetting where I come from. Also, when you are in a position of influence, you always, always remember to open doors for other people who might, because of discrimination or whatever, not be able to get that job. Because you are in a position of influence, and you can make a positive difference in your hiring decisions. That's what I decided to do.

Charles:

Well, for me, it's a vague memory. But what I do recall from being young is how many educators there were. So, I thought something must have been up. Daddy, aunts Addy and Ruby, they taught school. They taught for more than 40 years and Daddy for just about 50, I think.

So, there were these educators that we knew in our family, but I don't recall discussions about how all of that came about, and how they were able to even afford college. I just don't recall a lot of stories about it.

Percy Jr.:
Wow! Granddaddy had a lot of brothers and sisters who were also teachers.

Charles:
Yeah.

Percy Sr.:
Yes.

Charles:
Yeah. It was almost like it was in our DNA, and they were very successful in terms of wealth. They all did good in terms of movement up the economic ladder because of their education. They just believed that that was your key to opportunity. And they proved it just by looking at their lives that, by and large, they were all successful. All of them valued education. Uncle Oswald, for example, owned his own construction company, and he built a lot of homes. And Uncle Gary, he was an entrepreneur, he owned a lot of real estate, a retail business, a supermarket, and a service station. So, they all were successful, but it does point back to schooling. If I had to guess, it had to have come from their parents. I think you have to push that in your kids. That's just the way it is.

And you can almost guarantee that they got that from their parents because all of them really did well in terms of getting a good education. And they did well on the economic front. On the religious front, some of them were preachers, and all of them were Christians that believed in God.

So, you can see that common thread between the brothers and the sisters, *and they would visit each other on Sunday afternoons from the different towns they lived in across the Mississippi Delta.. They would all visit each other on Sunday and have dinner. And that was a way we kept the famiy together. So, yeah, it was powerful.*

And I think, Percy, on education, the question that you asked, I think for us, I think that whole educational arena, I think it was a lived experience. We saw it every day in our father, and we saw it in our aunts and uncles. And so, perhaps there was just no need for a lot of conversation about it because, for us, it was a lived experience. It was life. You were fully immersed in it.

Percy Jr.:

Now, all of this was going on in Jim Crow Mississippi, except for Uncle Percy, right? I think he went to Chicago, right? But for the most part, like Gary, Oswald, they all stayed in Mississippi, right?

Charles:

Yeah, but they did well in Chicago. They really did.

Percy Jr.:

Okay. Okay. That's good. We can move on to the next question.

So, I remember going down south as a child during summer break to spend time with the family, and both of you all talked about how Grandmother would always have a full-course meal, breakfast, and dinner, after going into the fields with you. And that was the case even when I was coming down there all the time, right? It was really never a day where she wasn't cooking a full breakfast in the morning and a full dinner at night. But I also remember the doors of the house being open for people in the community to be able to come in and sit down at the table and have a meal as well.

Was it like that even then, despite having, you know, a lack of resources, trying to feed eight within your own household? Was the family house open to the community back then, like it was when I was coming down there?

Charles:
Well, that's how I always remember it. And mother earned the reputation in the community as Mother Brown. Everybody called her Mother Brown. And so, beyond feeding a family of eight and the cost of that, we fed people in the community. We grew our own vegetables. We raised chickens and hogs, right? Pigs, per se. And so, she was able to do that when you might not be able to do that nowadays. And some of the kids would come back grown, and they would remember those experiences.

We'd be playing outside with our friends and when it was time to come to the table for dinner, they would come to the table and eat with us. It was like that every day. Our friends grew up not having food in their home and we carried them most days, and they would often talk about that. And then, even when we left and went off to college, you would have thought that our friends were no longer going to the family house for dinner or other kids, but that was not the case. There was a whole brand-new set of kids that we would come home and see at the family house, and they'd be sitting out on the porch like they were at home. They just took to Mother and Daddy because they knew that they were loved and they were fed and other things that they received from that home, that home away from home, almost like a community center.

So, I thought that was powerful. And you remember, not only children in the neighborhood, but Mother was very kind to pets. There would be a lot of cats around the house, and Mother would have to also feed them. But it was really important that I think about the day-to-day life of our mother. It was the day-to-day management of a household, six children, all the laundry, and just so many things to do, and she just did a superb job at all of that.

I never heard them complain. You mentioned Percy, about lack of resources. We weren't by no means rich, but I never did ever hear the word uttered out of my parents' mouth that we don't have enough food to feed us, and we all were heavy eaters. Somehow, they always had plenty of food for us as well as our neighbors. And so that's a mystery in itself. So, we'll leave that there.

But I do have a couple of things under my beliefs and values. Okay. The value of work. I worked as an educator for 46 years, or even longer than that. But even before that, I did a lot of fieldwork starting at age nine and earning 30 cents an hour, ten hours a day, under horrific conditions. But what it taught me was to value work. I did want to get that in. I also thought later in my life, too, that those long hours like that at age nine, ten, eleven and how that must have been a major violation of child labor laws, but none of that stuff came to mind until much later. That terrible experience really did help me to value and appreciate work and, later in my life, to be paid well for it.

And, of course, there's family. Now, we value equality and justice for all. That came out of Dad and Mother and the civil rights movement. We talked about education and religion. And then there's this last piece now, helping others in need, in great need in some cases. So, those are some of the specific beliefs and values that arose out of that time in my family life and community.

Percy Jr.:

I mean, to be nine years old, and when you say fieldwork, you're talking cotton fields, right? You're talking about chopping cotton.

Charles:

Yes,

Percy Jr.:

Okay, so being an African American child in the Mississippi Delta in the '50s and '60s, you're chopping cotton. Let's talk about that a little bit. What was that experience like from your recollection?

Charles:

The days in the fields? Well, it was just absolutely hard. We'll work from five o'clock in the morning until four in the afternoon. You were paid at the end of the day in cash, three dollars. And the hot burning sun. Without any kind of benefits, you're out in the fields, and so you were subjected to poisonous snakes, and thank God I was never bitten by a water moccasin or rattlesnake, but certainly, in those fields, there were dangers such as that. But we didn't have any health insurance or any kind of protection if anything bad happened to us while we were working. So, it was very difficult—no benefits, no paid Social Security. And I used to say in speeches that I gave over the years that it was pretty close to slave labor as far as I'm concerned, but it was very, very difficult.

The adults who were trying to manage families versus a kid that was ten years old, and you are paid the same wage. In some cases, I remember when we did have to sort of help Dad pay the bills. You remember that, Percy? You may want to expand on that.

Percy Sr.:

Yeah, I was there.

Charles:

We worked to help Dad because times were really tight when we lost our supermarket and home and had to move away, and move back. Yes, it was very difficult. The work life.

Percy Jr.:

In the Delta at that time, were you all just part of picking and chopping, or were you also planting? So, you plant in the spring and—

Percy Sr.:

We chopped cotton. We did plant some of our own vegetables.

Charles:

And we raised livestock, like I said.

Percy Jr.:

So, you didn't have to work in the fields during the planting season? It was just the picking season?

Charles:

Not just the planting season, but beyond cotton, we picked okra and pecans and corn, wild greens. So, we made a little bit of money in that way, too, but it wasn't very much. I think a pound of pecans, we were only paid like 15 cents, if that's about right, Percy.

Percy Sr.:
Yeah.

Charles:
And some of these experiences are so difficult and painful that you almost want to forget some of them. I'm going to expand just a little bit on that, and then I'm going to talk about some other sources of income that we had for work. But as hard as it was out there in those cotton fields, going back to those values early on, the value of love, is what carried the day. Because, while we were out there chopping cotton in the sun, we would still be laughing and talking with each other, playing games. And we had each other, not just the family members but our friends. And we would just be fellowshipping and talking. So, it was a way that we escaped all of that. And because there was so much love in our home, we weren't miserable people who would walk around with a hung-down head and sadness. We still were joyful in spite of that because what overpowered all of that was those things we talked about.

But the other sources of revenue we had, we always had the family grocery store that was built adjacent to our home. Going back to Mother, she ran the store as an entrepreneur. When we moved to Duncan for those two years, she ran a clothing store. She was certainly an entrepreneur in her own right, and they helped a lot of people.

Percy Sr.:
And then Daddy, even though he was an educator, a schoolteacher, he owned a construction company called Brown and Sons Construction. So, we would go around and work on houses, and do repair work. We never really made a lot of money, and we often complained to Daddy, but because Daddy knew all these people, he always just helped them because they didn't have the money. And he was truly blessed for that in

so many other ways. And the other blessing for us was learning to be a carpenter. It's a great way to build character. William and all of us. Our brother William learned carpentry so well that he was a very successful real estate owner who would buy up real estate. And he would not only rehab homes, but he built homes. And all of that came from the skill of knowing how to be a builder.

And I knew a lot of things about carpentry as a child, but I didn't keep it going because, when I left and went to college, I forgot a lot of that teaching. But I did remember a lot of gardening skills from childhood. I kept up with my gardening skills and when I built my first home in Wisconsin, I always would garden and personally remember that in the backyard here in Wisconsin. I always had a garden, and I would grow tomatoes, other vegetables and varieties of greens and freeze them over the winter. And my kids, to this day, they loved a lot of those vegetables that we would grow in the garden. In today's terms, the vegetables I grew are considered organic.

So, that was basically the gist of the work part that Charles touched on. That's basically how we made it on the financial front. But I want to say as a closing on this section here that growing up in Mississippi, we were certainly poor, whatever you want to call it. But I really can't overemphasize the point that what we had going in terms of our values and the love—we had a lot of love. And at the end of the day, love carried the day because we were a happy family. We were happy. We played a lot. We went to church a lot. And so, the suffering or either being the oppressed people, it was there, and it was real, but because of the strength of each other and the community coming together, that enabled us to be able to persevere through all of that. We could draw that kind of strength from each other like that and have that strong emphasis on faith in the foundation of love. As a community today, some of those values we talked about, have been lost through the generations.

. . .

Charles:

I just want to add... I'm not sure if I realized that, at one point, we were not well off or that we were living in poverty. But prior to our house burning down and our supermarket, though, I think before all of that, though, and Dad being a teacher in the community with a full-time job, I think that we were middle-class African Americans in Rosedale at that time. Would you agree with that, Percy?

Percy Sr.:

Yep, I agree.

Charles:

So, we weren't always poor, but we had a crisis with the home burning and the supermarket, and the family never got back on its feet. In fact, I'm not sure we ever got totally back on our feet, but Dad had continued to work hard. I remember Dad walked from Rosedale to Duncan. And what is that, Percy, 14 miles to interview for a teaching job? So, he was very serious about getting back on his feet, getting his family back, and keeping us as a strong unit.

But I did want to get your views, Percy. Our economic status pre- and post-losing our property and the store.

Percy Sr.:

We lost everything we had to the ashes. There were four houses that burned down to the ground because we didn't have running water. They ran this water hose almost a mile down the road, and the train came along and broke the hose. And right after we lost our house and all of our property, the Black superintendent and school board fired

Daddy because they said he was teaching and advocating for school integration.

So, like Charles said, Daddy got the job in Duncan, Mississippi, and we moved there for two years. And for one of those years, the house that we lived in up until recently, the family house, was built back largely with the help of Uncle Oswald, who would come in on Sundays and bring about 15 workers, and they would work for free as a gift. And then all of the materials, he would get that, and he just gave that at a discount. So, yeah, we built back from the ashes.

But the last thing I want to note about what it was like growing up in Mississippi. You'll see these signs saying color only, white only. You go to the movie theater, you'd have to sit up in the back of the balcony on the old, hard benches. The whites would sit downstairs on the first floor.

When you observe restaurants, you'll see the color-only signs. The white facilities would be nice. So early on, you'd see, and you go all across town, we would call it the white folks side of town, and you would see those nice homes with running water, lights, indoor toilets, and we didn't have any of that. So, you could quickly see that it was a lot of wrongs that needed to be made right. I mean, you could not ignore that growing up, that there were a lot of wrongs that needed to be addressed, and I'll stop at that because I know we're gonna get into that more.

Percy Jr.:

So, yeah, that's actually leading into the next question, right, which is, what did it feel like growing up in a time when racial inequality was the law? Jim Crow, you talked about the bathrooms, colored only, white only, the movie theater, they got you all the way up in the balcony with no air. Do you remember, like, how old were you when you started asking yourself, what is this? Or was it just hard to remember? Was it *five, six years old? Do you remember playing with white kids growing up? Or was it that segregated where there was no crossover whatsoever?*

Charles:

No, I knew that we were viewed as second-class citizens as a child. I knew there was not equality, but the difference is our family did not accept it. We rolled up our sleeves and got to work and said, "We're going to bring significant change around some of these issues." Not only the Black and white theater, but you had the white and Black section of the hospital. You had the Black and white section of town. You were not welcome at white churches. You could not go to a white swimming pool or baseball diamonds. You could not be buried in a white cemetery. So, it was clear. And we made a commitment to take some of these issues on and bring about change.

School Desegregation, Civil Rights Activism, and Intimidation

Percy Jr.:

The Brown family decided to enter the all-white schools in Rosedale when they allowed it for the first time in 1965?

You are leaving the teachers that live in the same neighborhood as you. They went to the same church as you, and they were also educating you.

Charles:

Yes.

Percy Jr.:

And the Brown family decided, in the spirit of racial equality, to give that up, to go into an all-white school system in Rosedale, Mississippi, in the 1960s, right?

And I know it was more than just getting your education, right? Because y'all were trying to bust up Jim Crow laws and to force Rosedale to abide by the law in the Supreme Court decision.

Like, what was going on in y'all's mind knowing that you were about to, you know, remove yourself from that dynamic a little bit where those teachers now are not going to be your teachers? You will still see them in church, but now you're going into the white school unless they hired some of the Black teachers. I don't know if they did or not. Y'all can answer that. But what was that transition like? I mean, was it overwhelmingly supported? Or were there people in the Black community or teachers that were, like, why are y'all doing this? Why are y'all going to the white schools? Since we're talking about education, right?

Charles:

There was some resistance to it, but if you go back to those Black teachers you're talking about, well, the education at the Black school was substandard. So, when I transferred to the white school, I was getting a better education. There were better resources, better books, and supplies. Did you feel like you lost the love from them, like did you feel the love from white teachers like you felt from Black teachers? No, I did not. There were some good white teachers, and we did not necessarily receive love from all the Black teachers.

But I was on a mission to change this second-class citizenship.

Percy Jr.:
It was a hostile environment.

Charles:
Every day was not a good day at the white school. But I think to do nothing and to stay segregated would have brought more harm, I think, to our rights.

Percy Jr.:
Like, knowing you ain't gonna have your friends at school, like, that had to be a lot.

Charles:
Well, we still had our community and friends because, when we returned home from school, you returned back to your community. That's right. And weekends and evenings, you still had all of that going. But for us, it was a matter of principle that just the fact that somebody told you that you cannot come to this school because I'm Black. Because of a law, you cannot come. So, that was the driving force. It was the principle of it that we felt that we should be able to go to any school. We could either go to the Black school, and a lot of people chose to stay at the Black school—and let me point this out—because they were intimidated and afraid. Because they knew if they took their kids up there to that white school, they might lose their job or even their life. So, there were some Blacks that did not want to go. They didn't want to go because they were afraid, they were intimidated that if they did that, they would lose their job.

So, the point we wanted to make was that, hey, we have a right to go to this school. That's a right, and you denied us a right. That was the main motivator, but like you say, we did end up getting a really good education. They had new books instead of old books that were passed down. So, we did gain a lot by going to the white school, but there were definitely some Blacks who did not want to go for different reasons. They were fine being in that Black setting, but some were afraid. See, just like with all these other things, fear and intimidation was rampant. For example, trying to get people to sign petitions advocating for their rights. People would be afraid to sign those petitions. Some would sign the petitions and come back to Daddy and say, "Take my name off," because they were threatened by their boss or somebody said, "I'm going to fire you."

Percy Sr.:

So, during Jim Crow, you always had violence, and the threat of intimidation was always there. And you knew that that's the price you would pay. We dealt with the threat of churches being bombed if civil rights meetings were being held in a church, or a cross being burned in front of your home by the KKK, which symbolized that in 24 hours, they were going to bomb your home. All of those things were designed to intimidate you. And that's why you have to—I think Charles mentioned that coming back to those values of courage—you have to have in you a degree of courage and strength to say, "You're not going to back down." I'm not coming at you in a violent way because we were part of the SNCC, the Student Nonviolent Coordinating Committee, so we didn't embrace violence. But we were courageous, and that goes back again. It's always going to come back to that question of what are the values that you hold and the beliefs that you hold.

Percy Jr.:

So, for the reader, what were some of those forms of intimidation that y'all actually experienced in that era of Jim Crow, before and during your involvement in the movement?

Charles:
 I just want to quickly deal with the Parchman (Prison) experience. It was not unusual that we would have all of these rallies, adults and children alike, and in order to have a march or a demonstration, you needed a city permit. Usually, we did not have one. I think we did get permits, which might not have been issued. It made no difference whether you had a permit or not; all these terrible things could happen to you. Marches and rallies were forms of civil disobedience, which is a way to participate in the political process. Those who participated in marches and rallies, children and adults alike, were shot at and fired from their jobs. There was one time when we were jailed for civil disobedience in the local jail in Rosedale and subsequently transferred to a maximum security prison to stay overnight. And on the way there, it was terrifying, being on that bus, it was a Black bus, I'll never forget, on that bus, and as I could look out the window and look behind, there was a trail of cars and pickup trucks. And I would think, you know, they must be the Ku Klux Klan. Well, who knows? I don't know, but I was terrified as a, what I believe, maybe a 13-year-old. Well, they got on the bridge over the water and just stopped and stood there. So, my thoughts as a child: This is the end. They were going to drive the bus over the bridge, so that kind of intimidation.

 When we got to the prison, they checked us in, gave us various clothing to wear, made us drink laxatives and milk of magnesia, turned up the air or turned down the air, whichever one, to make it colder on metal beds. Now, that experience, I will never forget. It was horrific. It was terrifying.

. . .

Percy Sr.:

So, when you brought that word up, intimidation, right away, what came to mind was that bus ride to Parchman Prison, that I wanted to have an opportunity to explain how intimidating that was. And then, when you went back to the community, you were still marching in protest.

Charles:

That's right. And I do want to add one other thing, Percy. It doesn't have to do with intimidation, but some have asked me after I've given speeches, "Well, why didn't your father sue these people, go to court?" And I would explain to them, "You're talking about white juries and white attorneys and white judges, and you're not going to get anywhere." So, there you go with another form of discrimination. But I did want to deal with that intimidation piece. That was horrifying, terrifying.

Percy Sr.:

And while we were on that bus, on that bridge, it was scary because they could have run the bus off of the bridge. And they knew that because they parked there a long time. Lines of cars and trucks were behind the bus, and that brought about the real fear of death. And what we did was we started singing those civil rights songs. "I'm not going to let nobody turn me around." "This little light of mine, I'm going to let it shine." And again, what kept us going was going back to the spiritual foundation of singing those songs on that bus and just clapping our hands. And that was our source of strength.

So, that was a great form of intimidation. And the other form of intimidation was when we held civil rights meetings and rallies. So, we needed a place to meet and hold rallies and things like that. And the best place, of course, was the churches because we didn't have community centers, but we had the church and Black pastors. Many of the civil rights leaders were pastors, but it was hard to get pastors to open up their church because they were afraid that they would be intimidated, or somebody would bomb their church because they held civil rights meetings. And I know it was some of the local churches, some of the leaders at Gospel Temple, where we attended church and even several pastors, who were very lukewarm to the idea of opening the church up for rallies and meetings. But because Daddy carried a lot of clout in the community and in the church, particularly Gospel Temple, it was the only church that reluctantly agreed to hold civil rights meetings.

We were dealing with intimidation, and that was a powerful weapon used to just frighten people, just scare them and constantly threaten them. They threatened to bomb your house or bomb your church. And we got that threat because, when we were the first Blacks to integrate into a white school, which was Rosedale Consolidated High School, The Ku Klux Klan came out that night and burnt a cross in front of our house, and everybody knew what that meant. That meant that in 24 hours, the house would be bombed. As the Klan members drove away, they fired two or three shots in the air right up the street from the house to let you know that they were ready to unleash violence on you and to scare you even further. So, the intimidation was real and as real as real could be.

Percy Jr.:

So the cross burning was a result of you all desegregating and going into the white school?

Percy Sr.:

And Dad being a civil rights leader in town, yes.

Percy Jr.:

Okay. So, y'all were going to the white school when that happened.

Percy Sr.:

And there were a lot of other things going on, too, because we were picketing in those white stores, holding back our business. And you mentioned here how old we were. When we were young, we would help draw up the picket signs and stuff. And when we were old enough, as a team, we would even wear picket signs right out there with the older people to help walk out.

And then we had, I think it was Ms. Nash—we got to confirm that —that came to Rosedale to help us organize what they called the Mississippi Student Union. That was our effort to work specifically with high school students to get them actually involved in the civil rights movement. And in Rosedale, we had it going in terms of our participation in everything, like Charles mentioned, the protests, the picketing, and all of that.

Charles:

Now, the only thing I don't remember that we were involved in as youth was the sit-ins. The sit-ins were kind of tricky. Maybe they thought that they were a little bit too dangerous.

Percy Sr.:

Yeah, we definitely did. Because you remember the restaurant and that theater? We went downstairs and sat down in the "whites only" section, which was the lower level of the white movie theater, and we went into that white restaurant that Miss Green had and sat in there. And usually, when you first go to those places, the first thing they would *do is just treat you badly. They might not even serve you most of the time. But they had to come around, but you had to go through all of it. And then we would deliberately go into the bathroom that said whites only or the water fountain that said white only. We would deliberately do those things. That's breaking down a barrier, but we always did it with a group. So, if they caught you, you may do a little jail time or whatever, but you were with other people and not alone.*

But all of this was going on along with growing up in that white school. So, it created a lot of anger. And they responded by doing things like what Charles talked about and taking us over the prison in Parchman, Mississippi... and then the KKK burning the cross in front of our home and things like that.

And then we got a lot of support coming in from up north, from Madison, Wisconsin. They would stay in our home, these Freedom Riders, and they would bring food to be distributed, and our oldest brother Morgan would pick up food from different parts of the country to be distributed. So, we brought in a lot of resources during that time as well to make sure people had food and other things.

Charles:

I want to deal with two more intimidating things just right quick. I guess in looking at these questions, there are two dealing with intimidation. And one of them was when I was in eighth grade and wanted to play on the basketball team. Mother and Dad did ask me to leave the basketball team because word got out that neighboring towns or schools were going to kill me if I showed up for a basketball game. Now, that might have been a bluff, right? And I think my parents, Mother and Daddy, had gone far enough, you know, in putting their children in harm's way. And I thought that might have been an unnecessary risk. So, I did leave the team. And all I was was a 13-year-old who just simply wanted to play basketball.

Another form of intimidation in the first year I went to the white school was when the bell would ring. The hallway was always congested. So, I would be in that congested hallway, and those white people would be kind of pushing me, walking on my heels. It was just so much physical harassment. I almost hated it when the bell rang. So, what I started doing was I would go exit the school, go outside, and run as fast as I could to get to the door to the entrance of where the other class was, just not to suffer that physical harassment. I will get into the building early. I'll be the first one there, and I'll go and take my seat.

So, there were many, many examples of this kind of intimidation, but it really did not; it never dampened my desire. In fact, it just heightened my motivation to keep going because it was just so bad. And the reason why is because I knew it was more than about me. We were doing it for a bigger cause. That's right. Something bigger. There was a nationwide effort going on at that time, and you were standing up for a cause. So, you had to represent that cause. You couldn't allow yourself to just take it personally and look at it that way. The more they tried to discriminate against you, the harder you worked in school because you had to prove that, look, I can come up here and show y'all I can be smart. And so, you worked hard. We came out at the top of our graduating classes and should have been valedictorians, but we weren't fully recognized as such. And that's a whole different story there.

Percy Jr.:
    So, real quick, I'm sure when you were in those white schools, there was social isolation for the most part from the rest of the student body. But were there any white kids that had some empathy or compassion and tried to connect with you all? And were there any teachers that you can say had some compassion?

Charles:

Yes. Well, I'll start with the teachers, and it'll be very brief on the students. I'll never forget. I don't know if Ms. Tullis is still living or not, but Ms. Tullis was my 11th and 12th grade English teacher. I don't know; I never could discern a bone of racism or discrimination in her. She wrote a letter for me to come to the University of Wisconsin-Madison. That was Miss Tullis.

I also want to highlight Miss Sissel. The reason why my math is strong today, was strong when I taught it, was due to the teachings from Miss Taylor and Miss Sissel. I never could discern any glimpse of racism or discrimination in her. Now, Ms. Taylor had a strong background, too, in math, and both teachers allowed me to lead discussions at the blackboard, working out complicated problems, both of those teachers did that.

Charles:

Yeah, Ms. Taylor. Now, there was something about her, and I think Ms. Taylor might have had a little bone of racism, but it was never belligerent. But I think she had the same level of expectations for us as Black students as she did for those white students.

Now, in terms of whether or not I had any student friends, well, there were a few white kids that I would talk to from time to time. They were just pretty okay. But what I told young people in speeches for at least two decades was that I did not have any friends at the white school.

Percy Jr.:

Okay. How about for you Dad?

Percy Sr.:

Even though a few of them you might have known beforehand, they were always cool when you saw them out on the street somewhere, but once you came to that school, it was like, "I don't know you." So, that was the big thing. You got nothing from those students at all. No words, no nothing. Charles already explained the teaching. But it was a tough nut to crack with those students to the point that you weren't getting anywhere with those students. Because, if you tried to sit at a table, you know, with an extra chair there and six or seven white students, they'll all get up immediately and leave when you come to sit there, or if you're in the assembly hall and you sit in an aisle, they'll all empty that aisle and go to another one. So, they will let you know, but you come to a point where you cannot allow that to get you down. You have to keep going. Oh, yeah, you have to keep going. You have to, for sure.

Percy Jr.:

And what about the Freedom Riders? I know I'm getting away from the bullet points, but I want you to share your experiences with the Freedom Riders.

Yeah, but if you can speak to that, right, since we're talking about the positive experiences that you had with some of your white teachers, those Freedom Riders were white students from UW-Madison.

Percy Sr.:

Yeah. We knew we were part of something bigger because—I think you also had this question, too: how did we find out about what was going on around the nation with the movement.... See, we were part of the Mississippi Democratic Party, the SCLC, the Mississippi Student Union, and SNCC. Sometimes, they would have representatives, and Ms. Nash, I think she's still alive today, would come to Rosedale and help us with organizations like the Mississippi Student Union. Dr. King, we never got to meet him in person per se, but we would keep up with the news.

He was an inspiration to all of us, his speaking and so forth. We were tied into all of that. I think that that kept us motivated and focused, that we were not in this alone. We were part of a bigger cause. And the civil rights leaders that were coming in from across the country, they reinforced that. Jews, whites, rabbis, and in particular the white students from the University of Wisconsin-Madison, they united and locked hand in hand with us and said, "We're going to treat y'all like our brothers and sisters." We took them home. They risked their lives because they were treated worse than we were sometimes. They would be called N-word lovers: "You N-lovers." They would be thrown in jail and at times beaten half to death. And some of them lost their lives.

So, it was a great risk. And that's how I found out about Madison and the university. They had an organization in Madison called Measure for Measure. And the white students who stayed with us were representatives of that organization. They would bring clothing down and big U-Hauls of food. But at the same time, they would be right there with us and marching and things like that. So that's when I got my first introduction to Madison, Wisconsin, and those very Freedom Riders. I ended up applying to the University of Wisconsin-Madison and was accepted. I caught a ride with them all the way to Madison. I didn't have any money to fly or nothing like that. So we rode in the back of a U-Haul truck, and they brought me right to my dorm, and I never looked back.

Oh yeah, I almost forgot. Fannie Lou Hamer used to always come up to Madison to give speeches and things. She was from Ruleville, Mississippi, not too far from where we grew up in the Delta. She was just down the road from us, so I saw her speak in Mississippi and Wisconsin... People loved Fannie Lou Hamer. There were so many amazing civil rights speakers and when they came to Rosedale, they were like celebrities. When Fannie Lou Hamer and others would speak to you, they moved you. They would energize you, like wow, and have you pumped up.

Percy Jr.:

And see, it seems like we don't have that type of leadership anymore.

Percy Sr.:

That's a problem.

Percy Jr.:

The Black community had powerful role models and leaders in the '60s.

Percy Sr.:

Yeah. That was really an important piece to that. And we kept up, though. I remember when Martin Luther King was assassinated. That very next day, I went to class in the white school, and they had a general session for a half-hour. And so, it was written on the blackboard in the classroom, "I'm glad that nigger is dead." The teacher, she came in, and she saw it there. And she didn't do anything about it. She just let it stay there, boy. And I was sitting there, already sad over Dr. King. Our great leader was gone. And you felt hopeless, you know, when you lose your leader, it almost sent you saying, "No, is this movement going to die?" All of our work, you know, went down the tube because he died. And I'm sitting there, struggling and all that, and then I'm looking at the big letters on the blackboard. And so, finally, after she's just seeing me *suffering, suffering, suffering, she finally erased it. But when she erased it, she then said, "Oh, who did this?" There was no apology for what I experienced. I mean, she should have come right in and said, "I need to deal with this because it's unacceptable."*

Percy Jr.:

Right. She didn't say a word, but personally, I'm sorry you had to go through whoever wrote this. But this was, again, clearly another form of intimidation.

Percy Sr.:

And I want to add one other thing. I know we got to move along. I don't think I realized when you brought up how the civil rights leaders per se used to come south and stay in our house and the cross burning. I don't think I realized at that time how dangerous all that was. After I was terrified that night by that cross burning, how I got up scared as hell and went to school the next day. Why didn't I go to Dad and Mother and say I just can't do this anymore? Or they could have thrown a bomb in our home because the Brown family has them nigger lovers down there, them civil rights people in their house. Those things never really came to mind. I was walking to school up and down that railroad track. They could have done anything to me.

Charles:

Yeah, they could have killed us, and nobody would have known who did it. They had many opportunities, yes.

Percy Sr.:
Literally many opportunities.

Percy Sr.:
We walked that railroad track.

Percy Sr.:
But Percy Jr., the story is so long that you can barely give justice to it in a two-hour Zoom or whatever. There is a lot, but at least we're giving a glimpse of what those days were.

And on that question, personally, of what role Daddy had in the local movement, I already touched on a little bit when I said that he was a leader in that he got the church to hold civil rights meetings. Gospel Temple was the church. It was located at the fork of the street, perfect for a rally. It had those high steps so the speakers could be up high and then all that space on the side. You could get a lot of people there. But Daddy himself put it on the line for that.

And Daddy was very active in picketing, and he really led the way on those petitions. Daddy was an educator, so he could write the demands up in a powerful way and demand these things, the light and running water and infrastructure, pavement, and better sewer and all that, because we had outhouses at that time.

Now, one thing that was scary for Daddy was that he would be picketing late at night. At ten, eleven o'clock at night, everybody else would be going home, and Daddy would be still, you know, in front of Charlie and Sam grocery stores. He would still be wearing that picket sign. And then, when he finally decided to come home, he'd walk that long, dark road by himself at night. Somebody could have grabbed Daddy and thrown him in a car and taken him over the levy to the Mississippi River to kill him and dump him in the river. But somehow, the hand of God was with Daddy, so no harm, hurt, or danger came up against him.

I still think about that a lot today. And I get tears when I think of it because Mother would sometimes get on Daddy and say, "You need to have somebody else to pick you up and drive you home. Or when everybody else has gone home, don't stay there by yourself until the store closes because it will be too dangerous."

But Daddy played a large role in the local movement. He was an educator. He was very articulate and was the first person in the Mississippi Delta out front advocating for racial school desegregation. He was accused of teaching racial integration because he asked the question to students, will the day come when you will see marriages between whites and Blacks and white kids playing together? It's as if it came from Dr. King's "I Have a Dream" speech, yet the speech hadn't been delivered. That was too much at that time and he was fired from the all-Black school in Rosedale, Mississippi.

And that board was an all-Black board because it was an all-Black school. They fired him right after he had gotten his house burned down. They were Uncle Toms. Yeah, they were Uncle Toms because they knew that teaching racial integration was against the law in Mississippi and they were ok with that.

Daddy was looking into the future as a great, wise person. And he was way before his time. And if you look today, you see that a lot of that has come to pass, but he paid a price for that vision and dream that he shared. So, Percy Jr., that specific example would be another excellent example of what I meant about Daddy being progressive at the time.

Outcome: The Life You Live
Because of Your Beliefs and Values

Percy Sr.:
In the bullet that you have here, please share a story or two about your role and its impact on you. Early on, when I was in Mississippi, I began to see... I could see all the wrongs, but I didn't have any sense of how to respond. So, as we grew older and as the opportunity presented itself, we figured out some powerful ways that we've already talked about that we were able to respond to. And how that impacted me was I was able to see myself as a difference maker because I knew that I would give up my time for the better good of the community.

I carried that with me when I came to UW, which was a very progressive liberal school where white students were protesting alongside the Black Power movement and the Vietnam War. And I was out there at all those marches and everything. So, it really did impact me.

And then it impacted me in another way. I ended up pursuing an MS degree in urban and regional planning because of all those infrastructure problems and housing problems and pavement and lighting, city planning kind of issues we had to deal with growing up in the Mississippi Delta. I said, "I want to return back to make it better for people's conditions, particularly in housing." And so, when I worked for the city of Madison in the Department of Housing and Urban Development, most of my big projects were revitalizing neighborhoods across Madison. I turned around and transformed whole neighborhoods out on Broadway, Simpson, Allied Drive, South Madison, and several other city neighborhoods.

I also pushed homeownership programs for first-time home buyers; I was able to do some great things. But what inspired me was I saw all those wrongs when I was young, and how I responded through the movement. Servant leadership was planted in me and it continued when I came to Wisconsin for college. I continued that. And then all that part about looking beyond just you and thinking about the community. I have always served on boards and committees in the community because it started right when we were so young. We were always in the 4-H club. We were always on different boards and committees that I served on.

That was how it made an impact on me. It looked like it clearly had the same impact on you, Charles, from looking at how active you've been.

Charles:

Yeah. I guess I'll just go to that. Because I think I've shared quite a few stories, but I want to go to that last bullet and what ways did the movement impact your overall well-being as a child and into adulthood. It made me become a lifelong advocate even today for civil rights and equality and to value service.

All these years, and I'm doing one today on Zoom and how it is so important to never stop. I was trying to hold back emotions and tears throughout this interview, but I got all the way to the end and it's still overwhelming.

And to tell this story... I don't speak like I used to, but I'm gonna keep telling the story. I told the story. My two daughters, Christina and Monica heard the story when they were young many, many, many times. And then, praise the Lord, I was able to still live and give these speeches. Well, my grandson Jason, he's heard the story more than once. And then maybe I won't be here for Malik to tell the story, but then his mother and his brother Jason, because they've heard the story, will be able to tell him also.

And then lastly, you know, this is hard and difficult and important work. My experiences in the movement just really helped me to realize how important diversity and inclusion is and that we all have rights that need to be respected and valued. So, I'll leave it at that.

Percy Jr.:

The one we skipped that I want to really make a strong point on was: how were you able to maintain a spirit of love in the face of hate and violence? I think I know the answer to that.

Percy Sr.:

We really all know the answer to that.

Charles:

I think I do, too. I'll let Percy answer that one.

Percy Sr.:

We talked about that foundation of love at the very beginning when Percy asked the question about values. That love, man, that love is powerful because the Bible says love overcomes evil. You know, love covers a multitude of sins, you know. Being Christians, you know, we look at the model and the teaching of Jesus. When he was even on the cross, he said, "Father, forgive them, for they know not what they've done." And he loved us so much that he gave his life up.

So, for us, you know, we believed in the nonviolent movement that Dr. King believed in. Had we picked up weapons and resulted to violence, we would basically be engaging in self-destruction. And somehow, we had that right. You know, of course, there was plenty of times when you would say to yourself, "Oh, I could just take him and wring his neck," but you just wouldn't go there because you had that strength to know that if you bow down to anger and you allow that hate to succumb you... And there were many civil rights leaders that I knew personally who allowed the hate that they experienced to overcome them, and they turned to heavy alcohol and drugs, and it basically destroyed them completely.

So, in the spirit of love, the more they would hate us, the more we would love, and in the end, it made me personally a more compassionate person in every aspect of my life. I always carried compassion as a value with me because I never wanted to see anybody else ever go through the hell and discrimination I went through. So, even when I served my 35 years with the city of Madison, I was a compassionate servant leader. I led with compassion because I knew that hate was not the way, and I didn't want to see anybody experience the hate I experienced.

So, it drove me to be the opposite of hate and to be a person that always showed love because love is more superior to hate and violence. Maybe if we were to turn into violence, maybe some of us might have gotten killed or something like that. You never know. But we always somehow maintained our cool because we are a family rooted in the core values of faith, love and education.

Despite the passing of two uncles and the continued life of my aunts, their legacy in the Civil Rights Movement lives on. The eldest, Morgan Brown, Jr., relocated to Wisconsin, where he worked for General Motors while raising a family. My uncle William chose to stay in Rosedale, where he built a successful investment properties business. Ella, my aunt, was the first Black person to desegregate and graduate from Rosedale Consolidated High School. She remained in Mississippi, serving as the City Clerk for Rosedale, Mississippi. and becoming the first Black woman to run for the County Chancery position in Bolivar County. She now owns her own tax accounting business. Lastly, my other aunt, Willie Mae lives in Wisconsin and owns a daycare.

Inspired by the white Freedom Riders from the University of Wisconsin-Madison, my father applied to the university and enrolled in the fall of 1969. My uncle Charles followed and enrolled at the university when he graduated from Rosedale Consolidated High School. They were involved in the Black Power Movement on campus and protested against the Vietnam War. They also became members of the Omega Psi Phi Fraternity, Inc., a predominantly Black fraternity as undergraduate students on campus. My father worked for the City of Madison in Housing and Urban Development for 35 years and has over 40 years of service as a deacon at Mt. Zion Baptist Church, the same as my grandfather. My uncle Charles taught adult basic education at Madison Area Technical College for over 45 years, as he followed my grandfather's career path.

They are men of service who practiced what they preached. The spirit of service to others from the time they were children throughout their adult lives has allowed them to transform the lives of many from the Mississippi Delta to Madison, Wisconsin. I have seen their service in action and its impact on the Madison area. My uncle Charles was recognized for his service by receiving the Martin Luther King, Jr. Humanitarian Award for the city of Madison and Dane County, Wisconsin. My father also received recognition for his service at the national level and received an award for revitalizing one of Madison's toughest neighborhoods. More importantly, so many people across the Madison area have shared with me their personal testimonies about how my father and uncles Morgan and Charles impacted their lives in a transformational way.

On August 30, 2008, community members from Rosedale, Mississippi, recognized their service in Madison and the Mississippi Delta. My grandfather, Professor Morgan Brown, and the rest of the Brown family received a resolution from the alumni of

Rosedale West Bolivar High School 1952–1970, recognizing them as civil rights heroes and pioneers in the field of education in Rosedale, Mississippi, and Madison, Wisconsin. This resolution is a testament to the value system of my family and how it can transform lives for the better. Lastly, it acknowledges the roots of who I would become in the next generation of the Brown story.

My great-grandparents Morgan Brown and Eliza (Holden) Brown.

My grandparents Morgan and Willie Mae Brown.

Percy Brown, Sr. high school graduation picture.

Charles Brown high school graduation picture.

Gospel Temple Church (Civil Rights meetings and rallies were held there).

William Brown, Morgan Brown, Jr., Charles Brown, and Percy Brown, Sr. (uncles and father, left to right).

Morgan Brown, Jr., Willie Mae Brown, Charles Brown, and Ella Mae Johnson (Brown siblings/uncles and aunts, left to right).

STRENGTH THROUGH GENERATIONS

Percy Brown, Jr. at three years old.

Percy Brown, Sr., Morgan Brown, Sr. and Percy Brown, Jr. (left to right).

Charles Brown, Latise Brown (sister), Percy Brown, Jr., Virginia Brown (mother) and Percy Brown, Sr. (left to right).

CHAPTER 5

"Education is the passport to the future, for tomorrow belongs to those who prepare for it today."
~ Malcolm X
Speech at founding rally of the Organization
of Afro-American Unity on June 28, 1964
Overview of Black America: 1968-1990

In November 1967, Dr. King announced the Poor People's Campaign at a staff meeting for the Southern Christian Leadership Conference (SCLC). The goal was for King to mobilize an initial group of two thousand people to organize and strategically go to Washington, D.C., Northern cities, and Southern states to start demanding jobs, fair pay for work, and more vital education for all poor adults and children regardless of race.

By this time, King's leadership had expanded beyond Black civil rights and became inclusive of all Americans. King also decided to protest the Vietnam War despite his co-leaders within the SCLC going against it. In 1967 and 1968, King delivered two powerful speeches, "The Three Evils of Society" and "Beyond Vietnam." King's message in these speeches leading up to his assassination on April 4, 1968, was far different from his famous 1963 "I Have a Dream" speech on the National Mall in Washington, D.C. King was no longer hopeful about the future of America. In an interview on NBC in 1967, King said that his dream, in many ways, had turned into a nightmare.

Months after Dr. King was killed in 1968, Robert F. Kennedy, the presidential candidate and brother of slain President John F. Kennedy, was also assassinated. Moreover, the Civil Rights Bill of 1968 would be the last piece of primary civil rights legislation passed in Congress for decades. King's assassination rocked the nation and would mark the beginning of the end of the nonviolent approach to civil rights activism. The movement shifted from non-violence and seeking integration and harmony with white Americans to Black self-empowerment, known more commonly as the Black Power movement.

The Black Power movement, which emerged as a response to the limitations of the nonviolent approach, focused on self-love or Black pride, establishing political institutions, and economic empowerment. This significant shift marked a departure from seeking integration and harmony with white Americans to a more assertive stance of Black self-empowerment. Organizations and people aligned with the Black Power Movement included the Black Panther Party, the Nation of Islam, Fred Hampton, Kwame Ture, Huey P. Newton, Angela Davis, and Shirley Chisholm, the first African American to run for president of the United States in 1972. The Black Power movement also made its way into higher education, where it was known as the Black Campus Movement. Across the nation, at predominantly white colleges and universities, Black faculty and students demanded the creation of an African American studies program and increased representation in the faculty. This movement began in 1965 and lasted until 1972.

Black Americans in the early 1970s, despite the ongoing struggle for their civil rights, continued to support the United States in the Vietnam War. The war, which lasted nearly two decades, finally ended in 1973. More than 300,000 Black Americans served in the Vietnam War, making up 25% of the Army's enlistment and 16% of the total armed forces despite constituting only 12% of the nation's population. This overrepresentation of Blacks in the military during the Vietnam War is a testament to our patriotism and love for the nation. However, it also highlighted the paradox of fighting for a country that did not fully recognize the rights and equality of Black Americans.

Captain Clifford Alexander, a Black American who fought in the Vietnam War, bravely stated to *TIME* magazine, "We are fighting over here against the Viet Cong and at home against discrimination... Together, we can win in both places." This powerful statement reflects Black Americans' unwavering resilience and determination, who continued to fight for their rights despite their challenges. Little did Captain Alexander know the extent to which war was being inflicted on Black Americans by entities of the government that he was putting his life on the line for in Vietnam.

On March 8, 1971, the Citizens Commission to Investigate the FBI broke into an FBI field office, stole several dossiers, and exposed the FBI's Counterintelligence Program (COINTELPRO) by sharing the documents with the news media. COINTELPRO was a FBI program, led by FBI Director Jay Edgar Hoover, that conducted illegal operations from 1956 to 1971. COINTELPRO aimed to disrupt and dismantle social movements that went against the status quo. Dr. King, Malcolm X, their organizations, and the Black Panther Party were heavily surveilled and infiltrated by the FBI to put their respective movements to an end. Though the program ended in 1971, by then, COINTELPRO had effectively disrupted the civil rights and Black power movements.

The collapse of the civil rights and Black Power movements left Black America vulnerable, a vulnerability that Hollywood would exploit in the early 1970s. Although Hollywood increased the representation of Black actors on the silver screen, it came with the perpetuation of stereotypes through blaxploitation films, or Black exploitation films. These films, usually low-budget and created by Black directors, used Black actors to tell stories that often revolved around drugs, sex, crime, and racism. Instead of attending marches or rallies to hear strong Black leaders, Black Americans who went to the movies saw themselves portrayed as pimps, criminals, and drug dealers. This negative portrayal is evident in movies like *Across 110th Street*, *The Mac*, and *Superfly*, all of which perpetuated negative and stereotypical images of Black people in movies.

By the mid-1970s, a shift began in which the portrayal of Black Americans on television was becoming more positive and not reinforcing stereotypes. Sitcoms such as *The Jeffersons* portrayed a Black family who came from nothing and worked their way to own a successful dry cleaning business and a penthouse apartment on the affluent East Side of town. Another popular sitcom was *Good Times*, which was about a Black family in the city of Chicago. Despite living in a low-income housing project, the love within the family, faith, and loving neighbors provided them the means to overcome the adversity they faced living in the so-called ghetto.

Bill Cosby created *Fat Albert and the Cosby Kids*, one of my favorite cartoons as a kid. There was always a lesson learned or a positive message for youth in the cartoon. By the late 1980s and early 1990s, Cosby expanded the positive portrayal of Black Americans with the popular television sitcoms *The Cosby Show* and *A Different World*. These shows provided a more accurate and positive representation of Black Americans, making the audience feel proud and represented.

Blaxploitation films and negative portrayals of Black Americans during the '70s were short-lived. Unbeknownst to most, something special was about to be born in New York City. I am talking about a culture that would emerge to become one of the most significant genres of music in human history. It all started on August 11, 1973, at 1520 Sedgwick Ave in the Bronx, and this newfound cultural revolution is hip-hop. Hip-hop had modest beginnings: DJ Kool Herc held a house party on Sedgwick Avenue, and he intended to create space to spread positivity across the neighborhood amid high rates of unemployment, heroin addiction, and slumlords burning apartment buildings for insurance money. Other Hip-Hop artists began to emerge on the scene, but it was Grandmaster Flash and the Furious Five who came out with a song called "The Message," which broke down the reality of what was happening in Black communities in the boroughs of New York and expanded the audience of Hip-Hop listeners.

I have taken high school students from Wisconsin to New York and always take them on the city's hip-hop tour. This unique bus tour comprehensively explains hip-hop's roots and evolution. The knowledgeable tour guides delve into the four elements of hip-hop culture: the DJ with the turntables, the MC or rapper with the microphone, breakdancing, and graffiti art. Tour guides also spoke about an unspoken yet crucial fifth element central to hip-hop in the early 1980s: knowledge of self. In its origins, hip-hop was about waking up Black America. According to hip-hop pioneer KRS-One, hip hop's roots and value system are peace, love, and unity.

Black America was rebounding from the crucial ending of the Civil Rights Movement. Through positive imaging on television shows and the birth of Hip-Hop, Black Americans began taking control over how we portrayed ourselves as a people. We were controlling our music and giving birth to a new genre of music. More importantly, we were continuing to make significant strides in education. According to the National Center for Education Statistics, college enrollment per capita for Black males was higher than for White males between 1980 and 1985. Moreover, from the 1970s to the late 1980s, Black students in public schools nearly closed the achievement gap with white students.

The progress Black Americans were making in the late 1970s through the early 1980s would come to a screeching halt under the Reagan administration. The Black community fell victim to the crack cocaine epidemic. While President Reagan and First Lady Nancy Reagan launched an anti-drug campaign during his administration called "Just Say No," an illegal arms trade was taking place, run by an entity of the government under his administration. This arms trade is known as the Iran-Contra Affair.

In the early 1980s, during the Reagan administration, most of Latin America was engaged in civil war, and a Marxist political wing took over Nicaragua. The U.S. government was working with and supporting a band of guerillas known as the Contras to try to create a coup against the Marxist Nicaraguan government. Congress eventually shut down the funding, so senior officials from the Reagan administration looked for ways to continue supporting the Contras.

The way they accomplished this was by secretly selling arms to Iran to fund and arm the Contras. In exchange, the Contras supplied U.S. government black operatives with cocaine, which they then distributed in the inner cities of the United States for cash. This black operation flooded Black communities with crack cocaine in the 1980s and 1990s, and the effects were devastating. I saw it firsthand as a child growing up in the so-called progressive/liberal Northern city of Madison, Wisconsin.

Personal Narrative: Growing up in Madison, Wisconsin

I was born on February 18, 1974, in Madison. My father attended the University of Wisconsin-Madison in the late 1960s and graduated with his bachelor's degree in 1975. On his birthday in 1975, my father married my mother, Virginia Brown. He would later go on to earn his master's degree. In 1981, my parents had my sister, Latise. My parents are devout Christians, and growing up we attended church every Sunday like clockwork. It was our extended family and a central part of my upbringing. My sister and I never went without, and for our parents, we were the priority. They cooked breakfast and dinner daily, and the only time we ate out was on a Friday evening at a local pizza restaurant, Paisan's. They were strict parents with high expectations, and whenever I got out of line, my mother was not afraid to give me a good whooping with the belt. I would not say I liked those expectations as a child, but as a man, I cannot thank my parents enough for all they have done for me, my family, and my sister. The love they showed me and my sister extended to the community through their service in the church and supporting immediate family members when they were struggling.

In addition to having two strong and loving parents with high expectations, I spent summers in Mississippi as a child and received that same love from my grandparents, uncles, aunt, and cousins. My three cousins Malcolm, Myriam and Henry in Mississippi are more like my sister and brothers. Henry, who is the closest in age to me, was the one I spent the most time with. We used to pick pecans, worked in Grandaddy's garden, and helped him with carpentry work in his homes. The summer I was 12 years old, my cousin Henry and I ran his parents' small grocery store without adult supervision. Imagine the responsibility placed on me and my cousin to work a store at 12 and 13 years old. I guess we were built for it because that summer, my grandfather taught me how to drive a car. I was receiving a well-rounded education from my family in Mississippi while developing a strong work ethic.

Back in Madison, the family I was spending the most time with were my dad's two brothers, Charles and Morgan, Jr. It was Uncle Charles who reinforced education in my life. He was an educator at Madison Area Technical College and an active member of the Omega Psi Phi Fraternity, Inc. His active involvement in the fraternity is what inspired me to pledge Omega. He took me to two national conclaves, and I was overwhelmed with excitement and motivation to go to college. Being immersed in a sea of thousands of Black men wearing purple and gold was mind-blowing. Not only did Uncle Charles expose me to the fraternity, but he also tutored me in math when I needed help. He was hands down a positive factor in my life. On the other hand, my uncle Morgan was a rolling stone. He was cool, a hustler, a ladies man, and someone who enjoyed the outdoors and playing basketball. I spent a lot of time with my uncle Morgan as a child. We camped, fished, played basketball, and went on miles-long bike rides. My uncle Morgan was street savvy, and spending time with him and his close friends, Bob and Frank, taught me life lessons that shaped me into an old soul.

Growing up in Madison as a Black youth was interesting. I was aware of race as a child because of things that I learned from my family and the Black church. However, I was utterly unaware of Madison's racial past and how it influenced the life experiences of Black Madisonians, including myself, during my adolescent years.

The city of Madison has a history of redlining. Redlining was outlining Black neighborhoods in red ink on city maps. Outlining neighborhoods on city maps served as a warning and discouraged banks from providing home mortgages and investing in those neighborhoods. This ultimately resulted in the devaluing of properties and overall communities for Black residents. Redlining practices also prevented Black residents from moving to more desirable neighborhoods with higher home property values. While Madison was expanding and building subdivision neighborhoods in the 1920s and 1930s, clauses in neighborhood covenants restricted Blacks from living there.

Not only was redlining a discriminatory practice in the Madison area, but there was great suspicion that the towns neighboring Madison were sundown towns. Sundown towns placed curfews on Black people. The expectation was for Black people to leave town or not be seen in town after the sun went down. If a Black person violated the law, they could be jailed or even killed. Another fascinating thing about the racial history of Madison was the existence of a sanctioned chapter of the Ku Klux Klan on campus at the University of Wisconsin-Madison in the 1920s. Lastly, the Ku Klux Klan held major rallies in Madison by the state capitol in the 1920s.

The history of redlining and other discriminatory practices in housing across the Madison area created racially segregated schools. Dr. Richard Harris writes about racial segregation in the Madison Metropolitan School District (MMSD) in his book *Growing Up Black in South Madison*. Harris writes: "In 1979, Sandra Solberg and Richard Harris, on behalf of two Neighborhood Centers, initiated a race discrimination complaint against the MMSD with the United States Department of Health, Education, and Welfare Office for Civil Rights (OCR). OCR investigated the past and present policies of the MMSD as they related to the status of the Lincoln Cluster Schools in South Madison. The complaint alleged that MMSD's decision in 1979 to close South Madison schools and redraw attendance boundaries discriminated against minority students and violated the Civil Rights Act of 1964. The initial OCR findings of probable cause led the MMSD to develop a school integration plan called the Midvale-Lincoln Elementary and Franklin-Randall school pairing plans" (History of MMSD).

The complaint was a result of a meeting between Harris and Solberg. Solberg met with Harris sometime in 1973 and shared information she received from a friend who was moving to Madison. Solberg's friend was looking for housing and inquired about a home near a Lutheran church because he was Lutheran. The realtor told him that it was not a good neighborhood because it was pretty close to a "Negro" area, and his children would have to go to school with them. This story is an example of how the real estate industry maintained racially segregated communities and schools despite laws restricting discriminatory practices.

The school pairing program in MMSD began in 1984. I was in fifth grade at Lincoln Elementary that year and was part of the busing program. I did not have to participate in busing to the west side of town, but there were kids from the west side, which was a more affluent side of town because of redlining, now coming to school with African-Americans, Latinos, Southeast Asians, and white students from blue collared families who lived on the south side. In hindsight, it was a transformational experience—seeing the effects of the Brown decision unfolding in Madison 30 years after the Supreme Court ruling in 1954. It also opened up opportunities for me to befriend white kids from the west side of town.

I remember my homeboy, Darren Paul, from the west side.

Hip-hop was growing, and one thing about hip-hop was the boombox—with the double-cassette deck and big speakers. Kids today might not know what I am talking about, but Darren had one, and it was the real deal. I envied Darren for having a boombox, and instead of being jealous of him, I befriended Darren, and we became cool. Darren's boombox was a powerful tool in building a community of friends. Two of my friends from the south side—Darren and my brother from another mother, Gus Doyle—and I started a breakdancing group called "Fantasy Crew." We had matching outfits, choreographed a show with Hip-Hop music, and had an opportunity to perform in front of the whole school, which was an extraordinary experience.

My brother from another mother, Gus Doyle, was from the west side of town; if I am not mistaken, he was the only Black kid bussed from the west side. Gus invited me to his house for his birthday party, and I said, "Wow! Nothing like this exists on the south side." His home felt like a mansion, and it opened my eyes to the socioeconomic differences between the west side and the south side of Madison. Gus is from a well-known family in Wisconsin. His father ended up becoming governor of Wisconsin for two terms. Our friendship opened up opportunities and afforded me experiences that would not have been available to me otherwise, and it was all possible due to the Brown decision.

I had a solid academic year in fifth grade, scoring in the 98th percentile on the California Achievement Test in reading and math and getting straight A's. I remember comparing report cards with my friend Curtis, and because I had all A's, he accused me of being white. At the time I had no idea what he was talking about. I would later learn that the comment from Curtis is an example of internalized racism, an internal belief of a Black person that they are racially inferior to whites. Because of my solid academic scores, Paul Bishop, who must have been a counselor at Cherokee

Middle School, placed me in advanced reading and math classes while I was in sixth grade. I was in those classes with one other Black student. I clearly remember being alienated from my homies in school. Some of my friends were segregated from the general education population and placed in self-contained classes because of suspected learning disabilities. I started to disengage from school because it was boring, I did not see myself reflected in the curriculum, and I was always the only Black male in my classes. While I had a Black teacher for third and fourth grade, that would be the last time that occurred in my K–12 experience.

I can recall two positive experiences in middle school. First, I met students from other elementary schools. While the school was predominantly white, there was a positive respect for one another across the student body regardless of race, ethnicity, or income. The second positive experience happened in 8th grade and was because of Paul Bishop. He encouraged me to join the forensics team, and I did. I decided to pursue the speech category, and I memorized Dr. King's "I Have a Dream" speech and competed in three speech categories. I won regionals and qualified for state in three categories. I took first or second place in the statewide competition in all three categories. This was the most memorable experience in middle school, and while the struggle was real most days at school, I always looked forward to being back on the south side after school.

Another aspect about growing up on the south side of Madison, which I talked about in previous chapters, was the importance of the Black church and its role in Black culture and the Black community. I was raised attending Mount Zion Baptist Church, the second oldest Black church in Madison. Several local civil rights activists were members of the church. Mount Zion was a tight-knit congregation that felt like family. It was indeed a village. I was being raised by more than my parents and family members. The church was raising me too. It was in the church that I began and started developing my public speaking skills. I performed in church plays, read scriptures from the Bible during devotion, read the church announcements, or, as I was able to do before graduating, delivered a quasi-sermon for youth Sunday. It paid off when I could use those opportunities on the eighth-grade debate team.

I also saw myself reflected in a positive light at church. Bill Cofield, the first Black head coach for the University of Wisconsin men's basketball team, was a deacon with my father at Mt. Zion. Richard Harris from the MMSD lawsuit was on the deacon board as well. Mt. Zion's membership included iconic local activists such as Betty Franklin Hammond, Pastor Joseph E. Dawson, Orlando Bell, and Rev. James C. Wright, who has a school named after him on the south side of Madison. Doctors, lawyers, insurance agents, teachers, and other professionals were also members. I was immersed in Black excellence at Mount Zion, which significantly influenced my identity development.

My most powerful experience in church as a child was seeing Jesus's image behind the pulpit; he looked like me. Images of Jesus and other biblical figures in America usually portray Jesus and the people of the Bible as European. Seeing a picture of Jesus that looked more like me than the images I saw of Him elsewhere left me with questions. I found the answer within myself. I found His reflection in me. The divinity within me is Him. This revelation pushes me to be the best version of myself. If you look at it that way, when you reflect on Jesus or the life of Jesus, it is more about seeing Him inside of yourself, but more importantly, it is about your daily walk in relationship to the world and humanity. I will acknowledge as a side note that in my mind and soul, I have replaced the image of white Jesus with one that looks like me. There is power in images. I believe this was part of strengthening my identity as a human being and solidifying my responsibility and commitment to treat all human beings in the way Jesus did.

I received so much love from the Mt. Zion church family, and it did not stop there. In addition to the Black church, the community had the Southside Raiders, an all-Black Little League football team in Dane County. I played for the Raiders in the 1980s, and I can recall Bran Foster and Justin Friske being the only white players on the team when I played. The Raiders were a dominant program because of the coaches. Will Boyd Smith, founder and head coach of the Southside Raiders, alongside his assistants, Jonathan Briscoe, Eugene Williams, and Rodney Abernathy, were fantastic role models. They drilled teamwork, a hard work ethic, and pride into every practice we had. Their expectations were high, and we were dominant. In three years, we only lost two games, and we shed tears when we lost those two games because we went into every game believing we would win.

Of course, the Dane County league managers always did things to make it difficult for the Raiders to be successful. For example, the Raiders played in the lightweight division, and at the weigh-in, I remember the coaches having issues with league officials. League officials questioned the ages of players, asked for birth certificates of players when it wasn't compulsory, and did other things that were not required to play in the league. The officiating on game day was sometimes questionable because there were no Black officials in the league. The coaches never made any excuses because they believed we could win regardless of officiating.

The church and the Raiders were providing me with everything I was not getting at school. These elements of my community were a foundation for learning, and it expanded beyond the church and the Raiders. I was also educated in hip-hop music. The first time I heard hip-hop was in 1980 or 1981, in Fort Lauderdale,

Florida, when I heard the song "The Breaks" by Kurtis Blow. I lost my mind and loved the song so much that my aunt Linda bought the record for me for Christmas. I cannot explain how "The Breaks" moved my mind, body, and soul. For me—and I heard this from a member of the hip-hop group Public Enemy—hip-hop is an acronym that means "higher intellectual powers for the healing of our people." What I mean by that is that the music and lyrics are soulful. At its roots, hip-hop is about uplifting Black people and speaks to the need to get to that fifth element of hip-hop: knowledge of self.

Artists such as Eric B. and Rakim, Boogie Down Productions with KRS-One, Public Enemy, X-Klan, Big Daddy Kane, the Jungle Brothers, De La Soul, and A Tribe Called Quest brought messages of uplift, positivity, and a call to action for Black youth to learn their history.

Growing up, accessing hip-hop music in Madison was challenging because the radio stations did not play it. A small radio station, WORT, had a show called "Saturday Soul Explosion," which came on at 11 p.m. and stayed on until about 3 or 4 a.m. I would stay up until eleven to press record on my tape deck to record the music from the radio show. I would be excited to see what they played, and I always got a few good hits. It was only in high school and getting a part-time job that I could go to the record store and buy cassette tapes and, in the early 1990s, compact discs (CDs).

It was cool being Black in the 1970s and 1980s. I grew up immersed in Black excellence. It was modeled in my family, the church, the community, and the music. The core values of faith, love, and education existed beyond my family. They were in the church and in my community. They were reinforced in every aspect of my life as a child. In addition to those core values, as a child I was bombarded with Black affirmations and learned about

Black history from my family and members of the Mt. Zion Baptist Church. I was rocking an afro, a sign of Black pride, as a toddler in the early 1970s and had a unique handshake with my dad called "Give me five on the Black hand side," another reinforcing message of Black pride. And while I was receiving the building blocks of developing a strong sense of self-worth from my family and community, I was also receiving an education on how to navigate America as a Black person.

I was learning what to do if I encountered law enforcement and had it drilled in my head that I'd have to work twice as hard to earn half of what white people have. This message implies that racism is real. I knew what they meant, and rather than being upset about it, I wouldn't let it stop me from accomplishing my goals. I was ready to fight racism if it got in my way. While it personally felt cool being Black growing up in the 1970s and 1980s, the Black male in America was under attack in the 1990s, and it was scary. This fear is different from the implied racism of "having to work twice as hard to earn half of what white folks have." Black American males in the 1990s were dealing with the wrath of the War on Drugs during the Clinton administration, a devastating policy and propaganda campaign that demonized Black American males and disproportionately targeted and incarcerated Black individuals, further exacerbating racial inequality in our society.

CHAPTER 6

"To be on a constant quest to be the best version of yourself. That's what the mentality is... It's a constant quest to try and be better today than you were yesterday, and better tomorrow than the day you were before."
~ Kobe Bryant

Overview of Black America: The 1990s

The 1990s began with a searing injustice for Black Americans. In 1991, Rodney King, a Black American resident of Los Angeles, California, was subjected to a brutal beating by four white police officers during a routine traffic stop. The incident, witnessed by several bystanders and captured on video, sparked widespread outrage when the officers were acquitted, leading to five days of riots in Los Angeles. What happened to Rodney King brought to the surface the police brutality that hip-hop artists such as Niggaz with Attitudes (NWA), West Coast rappers, made songs about years before the Rodney King tragedy.

NWA produced a controversial song called "F*** Tha Police." The song explains in detail how, in Los Angeles, white and Black police officers were engaging in police brutality against young Black males.

Even in filmmaking, Spike Lee, an African American filmmaker, released *Do the Right Thing* in 1989. The movie highlighted the complexities of racial issues between Blacks, Italians, and Asians in Black communities. Radio Raheem, a central character in the movie, was killed by New York City police officers. What ensued was a riot and significant destruction of businesses in the community. In many ways, NWA and Spike Lee were either prophetic, leading up to Rodney King, or bringing to light the reality of an ongoing adversarial relationship between the Black community and local law enforcement agencies.

In 1998, James Byrd Jr. was dragged to death behind a pickup truck for over three miles by white nationalists in Texas. Furthermore, in the 1990s, several Black churches across the South were mysteriously burned down, and no one was ever arrested or charged.

While the 1990s was a tumultuous start for Black America, we saw progress in politics, science, and sports. Kansas City and St. Louis, Missouri; Memphis, Tennessee; Denver, Colorado; Houston and Dallas, Texas; and Jackson, Mississippi, elected their first Black mayors. Carol Moseley Braun of Illinois was the first Black woman elected to the U.S. Senate. Colin Powell became the first Black Secretary of State under the George W. Bush administration. Regarding science, Dr. Mae Jemison became the first Black woman in space on the shuttle Endeavor. Tiger Woods broke the color barrier in golf while ascending to become the most recognized golfer in the world and was compared to Michael Jordan, the most celebrated and successful athlete in the 1990s. I was heavily influenced by Jordan's work ethic, competitiveness, and ultimate swag. His shoe line, Brand Jordan, transformed the meaning of sneakers, and his shoes are popular across multiple generations. There are young people today wearing his shoes who have no idea who he is. Today, I am still like a teenager and own dozens of retro Jordan sneakers.

Michael Jordan briefly retired from the NBA in 1993 after winning three straight championships, and nearly one year before his return to the NBA in 1995, one of the most significant criminal trials in American history unfolded, with race at its core: the O.J. Simpson murder trial. O.J. Simpson, a Black NFL Hall of Famer and Hollywood star, was accused of the murder of his ex-wife, Nicole Brown, and her friend, Ron Goldman, who were white. The trial, with its racial undertones, would leave an indelible mark on the nation's history, shaping the discourse on race relations in the '90s with its profound impact.

On June 17, 1994, Simpson was charged with the double murder. Later in the day, Simpson hid in the back of his Bronco truck while his friend drove in an attempt to escape on an LA interstate. Over 95 million Americans watched this live as all news stations were filming this attempted getaway. He later turned himself in and stood trial for the double murder. Johnny Cochran, an African American lawyer, served as lead attorney alongside a host of other attorneys, and in the media, they were called the Dream Team. The trial lasted eight months, and on October 3, 1995, O.J. Simpson was acquitted.

The O.J. Simpson trial was a turning point in race relations in the 1990s. For many Black Americans, it was not about the acquittal of O.J. Simpson. It was about justice finally tipping to our side for once, given the many times throughout American history that Black Americans never received justice for crimes committed against them by white Americans. The trial, with its racial undertones, was a stark reminder of the deep-seated racial divide in America. Too many times, white violence had gone unpunished, and in the rare instances when charges were filed, the perpetrators were often acquitted. This time, the scales of justice tipped to the other side, regardless of the truth. It was a moment that spoke volumes about America's racial landscape in the 1990s and the impact history has on the present.

Personal Narrative: The 1990s in the Midwest and Mississippi Delta

In the previous chapter, I mentioned the Iran-Contra scandal and the influx of crack cocaine into Black communities across the nation, including my hometown of Madison. While the Reagan administration allowed drugs to come into the country, it was President Bill Clinton, with the support of Joe Biden, who operationalized the war on drugs with the Crime Bill of 1994. This bill, often called the "Crime Bill," was a significant piece of legislation that profoundly impacted Black communities. It provided incentive grants to states nationwide to increase the number of police officers on the streets, provided local law enforcement agencies access to military-grade weaponry, and expanded the building of state and federal prisons if states enforced truth in sentencing—mandatory minimum sentencing of 85% of a convicted person's total sentence. The war on drugs, as enforced by this bill, disproportionately targeted and incarcerated Black individuals, leading to a generation of broken families and communities.

Drug laws at the federal level were unjust and racially biased. The federal cocaine law was based upon a hundred-to-one sentencing requirement for crack cocaine and powder cocaine. Five grams of crack carried a minimum of five years in federal prison, while 500 grams of powder cocaine carried the same minimum sentence. This is important because crack cocaine was inexpensive and considered a poor person's drug, whereas powder cocaine served as the choice drug for people from affluent backgrounds. It was easy to find a crack in any low-income community in America. It was in the big cities, mid-sized Midwestern cities, and the most rural parts of the Mississippi Delta.

Most people think the crack cocaine crisis and the war on drugs were limited to the inner cities. It was not, and I saw its devastating effects on the Southside of Madison. I saw a lot of good brothers and friends falling into the trap of selling crack. It was lucrative, and my friends were making fast money and plenty of it. I saw friends coming to school with five or six hundred dollars in their pockets that they made in a couple of hours, and they were buying lunch for everybody. Some of my friends probably made two or three thousand dollars a week. I am not condoning selling drugs, but it was very lucrative.

Consider being impoverished and while your mother is receiving government assistance, you attend a school system where there are not any Black teachers because the school district is predominantly white. You do not see yourself positively reflected in the curriculum, and you had zero support in school to help you get through. On the other hand, you can make six or seven hundred dollars daily as a teenager in the streets. I do not think race matters because anyone from a struggling background can fall into that, especially when you are 14 or 15 years old.

Low-income communities in Madison were the target of the war on drugs. When law enforcement was incentivized to increase drug arrests, they went into neighborhoods historically redlined or the south side of Madison. The Madison Police Department had an undercover sting operation called Operation Blue Blanket. The police department used U-Hauls and ice cream trucks to deploy undercover cops and use snitches to make drug arrests. There were police officers on the South side of Madison who got caught extorting drug dealers and violating the police code of ethics. While Operation Blue Blanket was in full swing on the south side, it was a different story on the west side of Madison or at the University of Wisconsin-Madison.

When I was in high school, I was a popular student. I was able to cross-navigate many communities in high school. I had my homies from the south side. My core friends during my teen and early adult years were Kedric, Garlon, Anthony, Myron, James, Tony, and Gus. We have been tight for over 30 years. In high school, most of us were athletes, and because of our friendships with white teammates, we were invited into predominantly white spaces outside of school. We were invited and went to parties hosted by white students from Madison West or graduates of West who were now college students at the University of Wisconsin-Madison. Madison West High School is in close proximity to the University of Wisconsin-Madison, a Big Ten college. These parties were unlike any party that was going on in my neighborhood. The white kids that we were cool with were having parties with barrels of beer. You got a cup for two dollars and could drink as much as you wanted. These types of parties never existed on the south side of Madison. On our side of town, it was all about 40-ounce bottles of beer.

Not only was there alcohol at the parties that my white friends hosted, but I saw drugs too. Cocaine was present at these parties, along with marijuana—and it was of a much higher grade than what I had seen on the south side of Madison. I also saw mushrooms and LSD, street drugs, which were not available on the south side.

Reflecting on that, I think about how, not just at UW Madison but even with my friends who lived in *affluent* communities of Madison, no one ever got busted for having drugs despite the evidence I provided. From my personal experience and knowing the history of Madison, it is clear how the history of racial discrimination influences present-day life.

Statistically, race plays no role in who sells or uses drugs more. It is statistically the same across racial lines, although the disproportionality comes in drug arrests.

The consequence of the war on drugs in Black America was the explosion of Black males being incarcerated for drug convictions. Many people do not talk about it, but when you are convicted of selling drugs, you become a second-class citizen. You lose your right to vote for some time or permanently. Moreover, you lose your right to access government-backed financial aid for higher education.

The consequences were steep for Black people who were convicted of drug offenses. Once released from prison, where do you start? If you wanted to go to school, where could you get the resources to do so? What supports were in place to help you transition from prison to mainstream society? When drug felons are released from prison, it is nearly impossible for them to build themselves back up. For example, some policies restrict a convicted felon from living with his wife or girlfriend with children if the woman received government assistance. This is one of the ways in which the Black family has been broken. People talk about the absent Black father without understanding how criminal justice policies make being an involved father extremely difficult.

I am not making excuses for anybody; I am just trying to offer a different perspective. However, you have to ask the question: If the federal government wanted to fight a war on drugs, why did they fight it on American streets? Why didn't they stop the drugs from coming into the country in the first place? Given what we know about the Iran-Contra arms deal, what happened to checks and balances in government? This was obvious government corruption that targeted the Black community and brought about the devastation of the Black family and community. Government corruption was never part of the narrative or dialogue in the media. The blame was placed on Black males and we were demonized and labeled by politicians and the media as "super predators."

During the 1990s and early 2000s, Blacks made up about 5% of the state population in Wisconsin but made up close to 50%, if not more, of the incarcerated population in Wisconsin. The majority of Black males who were locked up in Wisconsin prisons during that time were convicted of nonviolent crimes. They were jailed for selling drugs and possibly doing more time in prison than someone who was convicted of murder. So many brothers were going to prison that it scared the hell out of me. I cannot recall how many times I thought I might end up in prison. I could have easily gotten caught up in that because I had friends who were dealing; I could have been an accessory to a drug charge because I used to hang out with or be in the car with my friends while they were in possession of crack.

The trap of selling cocaine was one that I stayed away from. However, I had my struggles. I was completely disengaged from academics in high school. While I had the potential to perform at a high level, I could not get there. My parents pushed the hell out of me, and I knew I had to go to college. However, I still struggled. I was a popular student because I have an outgoing personality and was super social. I was voted on the homecoming court my senior year. In my freshman year, I was on the TWIRP (The Woman Is Responsible to Pay) court and was the only Black student represented on both courts. So, I had that piece, but regarding relationships with teachers, I often felt like they did not see me or my academic potential. Like in middle school, I was often the only Black student in most of my classes. I did have a few good teachers, but I wonder if I felt that way about them because I had a boy crush on them. It so happened that the attractive teachers also taught the classes I was interested in, business and DECA. I'm not sure if that is a coincidence or not, but it is hilarious in hindsight.

In hindsight, I believe I learned more from my peers in high school than I actually did in my coursework over four years at Madison West because I had cross-cultural relationships with different groups of students, whether it was the preppy white community or the goth community—there were so many different communities—I always tried to find ways to connect rather than see them as different. Culturally, I was different from the students I mentioned, but I did not see them as better or less than me. Instead, I wanted to learn from them. And that's what I did. When you go into other spaces and learn from people from different cultural backgrounds, it expands your worldview and makes you a better human being.

I graduated from high school in 1992 with a 1.97 grade point average. I scored well on the ACT and was automatically admitted to the University of Wisconsin-Whitewater. I bottomed out my first year at Whitewater and flunked out. I came back to Madison and went down a dark path. I got into the streets heavily and made decisions that could have dramatically altered my life. A close friend of mine got caught selling drugs and was convicted. Before he turned himself in to go to jail, his mom, a faith-going woman, wanted us to go to a church revival. I went with him, and the guest evangelist was a white woman from Texas. While she was praying, she started speaking directly to me and placed a prophecy on me. She said I would lead many people one day and that my friends would need to follow. At the time, I did not know what it meant, but I needed a glimpse of hope because I had hit rock bottom, and my parents were kicking me out of their house. I prayed for weeks, read *The Autobiography of Malcolm X*, watched Spike Lee's movie about Malcolm X's life with Denzel Washington playing Malcolm, and was led to write a letter to my grandparents in Mississippi, asking them if they would take me in. They said yes, and I wrote a check with no money in my checking account to pay for a one-way ticket on a Greyhound bus to Memphis, Tennessee, where my cousin Myriam lived. I stayed with her for a few months before moving to Rosedale, where my grandparents were. I ended up staying at my Aunt Ella's and Uncle Henry's home. They still had their small grocery store, so they also gave me my old job back from my childhood summer. Spending summers in Mississippi during my youth made my transition that much smoother. I was familiar with the community and had established relationships across the community.

It was a good thing that I moved because, not even a year after I left Wisconsin, my good friend Greg was murdered. We grew up together, joined Mt. Zion Baptist Church, and were baptized. He was a good brother who could have done amazing things but got caught up in the wrong things. Greg was murdered a block away from Mount Zion, where we were baptized together. It took the police department a while to find the murderer, and it was a high-profile case because Greg's uncle was a highly respected police officer for the city of Madison. It was so wild that my parents would not let me come home from Mississippi to attend the funeral. The murder was drug-related, and I cannot emphasize this enough: the war on drugs nearly decimated the Black community, and I do not think we have fully recovered from it.

It took only a short time to get focused when I moved to Mississippi. In the spring semester of 1995, I enrolled at Delta State University, 17 miles from Rosedale, where my father was raised. My cousin Henry was a student and football player at

Delta State when I enrolled in the spring of 1995. He showed me around campus, and his friends became my friends. The following semester, I made the Delta State basketball team as a walk-on, and in the fall of 1996, I pledged to become a member of the Omega Psi Phi Fraternity.

In my first semester on campus, an event called Old South Day was advertised. Being a Northern Black person, I asked, "What in the hell is Old South Day?" Old South Day was when all the white boys from the fraternities dressed up in Confederate uniforms, the white girls in sororities dressed up in Southern belle dresses, and they had this vast parade through campus, with Confederate flags waving everywhere and a giant pig roast at the end of it at our football stadium.

I was shell-shocked, thinking, *Man, the Confederate flag; is that not symbolic of slavery?* I asked my cousin and some Black friends, "What is up with this?"

They just replied, "That is their thing. That is their tradition."

That was eye-opening for me. One may think their attitude was lackluster, but it was not. As I would find out in the near future, my Black friends knew about the racial division and ongoing racial segregation on campus despite it being racially diverse. The following fall semester of 1995, O.J. Simpson was acquitted of the murders of Nicole Brown-Simpson and Ron Goldman. On the day of the verdict, I was in the student union with dozens of Black and white students. If you were a fly on the wall, you would have seen clear racial segregation in the student body. The white students were all together in one space, while the Black students were gathered in a separate space. We were all glued to the television to hear the verdict. When the judge announced that O.J. was not guilty, there was thunderous applause from the Black students and deafening silence from the white students. The racial divide in the country at the time mirrored our reactions to the verdict.

While on campus, I was active beyond basketball and the fraternity. I was also a member of the Black Student Union on campus. It was an active Black student union, and we did something special that I want to share. The university always had a homecoming court during the football season, and it was all female: two freshmen, two sophomores, two juniors, and two seniors. Every year, the students selected for homecoming court were girls from all-white sororities. In 1997, the leadership of the Black Student Union organized a campaign to change that.

First, the Black Student Union recruited Black girls to run for the homecoming court. Then, BSU members reached out to white students who were not part of the Greek network on campus and got them to vote for the female Black students. Seven out of the eight female Black students made the Homecoming Court. Oh, my goodness, that caused an uproar! We had media on campus, and the climate was extremely tense. At halftime during the homecoming game, the homecoming court was announced, and the girls were on the football field. Like the student union during the verdict of the O.J. trial, the stadium was racially segregated, and not one white person clapped for the Black girls who made the homecoming court. This was not a fight about taking something away but pushing for awareness and an acknowledgment that the campus was racially diverse and all things on campus should reflect that diversity. That was our little moment on campus, pushing back on the status quo.

Despite the racialized experiences on campus, I had an amazing time, met lifelong friends, and found purpose for my life. I fell in love with history. The dean of the history department, Dr. Allen Dennis, persuaded me to pursue a degree in history. My roommate, Nashid Madyun, and I were taking a U.S. history class with Dr. Dennis, and one day, he pulled us into his office to talk. Something about our writings for the class impressed him: the way we processed history and made connections to things today.

Dr. Dennis told my roommate and me that if we decide to major in history and get our master's degree and a PhD, we could write our own ticket because many universities lack Black professors in their faculties.

Nahsid told me several years later that he had lunch with Dr. Dennis. Dr. Dennis told him why he pulled us in and encouraged us to major in history. Apparently, after one of our exams, he thought that we were cheating. So, for the rest of the class that semester, he designed tests for me and my roommate that were more difficult than everybody else's. We were the only two Black students in the class, and we knocked those tests out and performed above his expectations.

Some people will say, "Well, that was racist." I did not know his motivation, but my relationship with him on campus was not like that. He was a loving man. He opened my eyes to the ways in which history has been distorted. While taking his course on the Civil War, I learned quickly that the Southern point of view is different than the Northern point of view. Most of us have learned that President Lincoln freed the slaves, but how many of us know that he believed in racist ideology? Dr. Dennis exposed me to Lincoln's beliefs when he had me read parts of Lincoln's debate against Stephen Douglass for the United States Senate. From that moment on, my critical thinking skills were enhanced, and I began to question everything. I would not be where I am today without my relationship with Reverend Dr. Allen Dennis because he saw something in me that I had not yet seen in myself.

The 1990s were challenging for me. I lost a few good friends to death. Many of my homies from the Southside fell victim to the consequences of selling crack. Overall, the Black community was under attack, and all I could do was thank God for sparing me. I was lost in the early 1990s, but by the time we entered the new millennium, I survived falling victim to societal traps and reinvented myself. I graduated from Delta State in May of 1998 with a bachelor's degree in history with a minor in political science and laid the foundation for a career as an educator and servant leader.

CHAPTER 7

"When machines and computers, profit motives and property rights, are considered more than people, the giant triplets of racism, extreme materialism, and militarism are incapable of being conquered."
~ Rev. Martin Luther King, Jr.
Beyond Vietnam Speech
April 4, 1967 at Riverside Church in New York, New York
Overview of Black America: 2000-Present

The new millennium began with the Y2K scare. People around the world feared computers and technology would completely shut down as we transitioned into 2000. That did not happen. However, major events occurred globally, particularly across the United States over the next two decades that would fundamentally change this country.

People of the Islamic faith in the United States became targets of Islamophobia in the aftermath of the 9/11 tragedy. President

George W. Bush passed new education legislation called No Child Left Behind (NCLB), placing tighter school accountability measures on public schools. For the first time, NCLB made schools disaggregate their data by race, and if schools were failing, they risked losing federal funding. NCLB had a tremendous impact on the public education system. In 2002, a Harvard Civil Rights Project (HCRP) report concluded that American schools were starting to resegregate again. The report found that schools were more segregated in 2000 than in 1970, when busing for desegregation began.

In 2005, New Orleans, Louisiana, and the surrounding shores of the Gulf of Mexico were devastated by a Category 5 hurricane. Hurricane Katrina made landfall on August 29, 2005, and the devastation was immense. New Orleans is a major city with a large Black population, and many of them resided in the Lower Ninth Ward. The Lower Ninth Ward was completely decimated by the storm. Approximately fourteen hundred people died, and thousands of Black residents were permanently displaced and scattered across the U.S. Katrina caused $180 billion in damage, and 80% of New Orleans was underwater for weeks. Black American filmmaker Spike Lee produced a four-part docuseries called *When the Levees Broke*, which gives a detailed and first-person account of the storm and its devastation and highlights the challenges faced by the Black community in the aftermath of the hurricane.

Days and weeks after Hurricane Katrina, concerns were raised about the speed at which the federal government was providing aid to New Orleans. Hip-hop mogul Kanye West made a bold statement during a televised Hurricane Katrina benefit concert, declaring, "George Bush does not like Black people." This statement was a direct response to the slow reaction of the Bush administration and FEMA, which seemed to prioritize Republican-voting communities while disregarding the city of New Orleans. West's outspoken criticism highlighted the need for swift and equitable disaster relief, particularly for the Black community in New Orleans. It didn't happen, and nearly two decades later, predominantly Black communities in New Orleans are still rebuilding.

Three years after Katrina, the nation nearly went into an economic depression. During the financial crisis of 2008, many Americans lost significant amounts of money from their 401(k) retirement accounts and equity in their homes because the housing market collapsed. There were millions of home foreclosures across the U.S. Unemployment skyrocketed, and Black Americans were disproportionately affected. The unemployment rate for Blacks was twice that of white Americans when the crisis hit, and it stayed that way for years, causing a significant loss of wealth and employment in the Black community.

According to the ACLU, "Home equity values for Black and white families at the same income and education levels were headed toward parity by 2050. Instead, the financial crisis has sent it in the opposite direction, and Black Americans will lose close to $100,000 in wealth by 2031." The financial crisis of 2008 disproportionately affected Black Americans due to a combination of factors, including predatory lending practices, higher unemployment rates, and the devaluation of properties in predominantly Black neighborhoods. As a result, the wealth gap between Black and white families widened, and this disparity will persist for years to come, highlighting the systemic issues that perpetuate wealth inequality in the Black community today.

Currently, white Americans have ten times more wealth than Black Americans. Whites, on average, have $171,000 of wealth compared to $17,000 for Blacks. The median net worth of college-educated Black families is $68,200, significantly more than the

$17,000 average for Black families and nearly five times below the $399,000 for college-educated whites. Black millennials have a homeownership rate of 17% compared to 46% for whites, and this gap is the largest since World War II. Statistics show over time that the politics of this nation—both liberal and conservative legislation—has done little to help Black Americans level the economic playing field.

Despite these setbacks, Black Americans have made progress. Although we have faced numerous challenges, we continue to move forward as a people, making significant strides in various fields. For example, between 1990 and 2018, college graduation rates for Black Americans more than doubled, a testament to our belief and value in education. In 2020, there were 56 Black members of Congress compared to 5 in 1964, a clear indication of our increasing representation in the political arena. The new millennium has brought forth a proliferation of Black athletes, authors, screenwriters, and others dominating their fields, showcasing our talent and potential. Black America has also grown its annual spending power from $15 billion in 1954 to a projected $2 trillion by the end of 2024, a sign of our increasing economic influence. Lastly, the U.S. did the unthinkable and elected its first Black American president, President Obama, who would win two terms in 2008 and 2012. Many Americans believed that with the election of President Obama, the nation became post-racial, ushering in a new era of hope and optimism.

However, midway through President Obama's second term, on June 17, 2015, Dylann Roof, a white supremacist, went into Emmanuel African Methodist Episcopal Church in Charleston, South Carolina, and killed nine Black people and injured a tenth. This is one of many tragedies Black Americans have been forced to deal with over the last decade. For the first time since Rodney King, we witnessed video-recorded executions of Black Americans by white police officers. Michael Brown, Eric Gardner, Tamir Rice, and Laquan McDonald are but a few examples of the many deaths that the world witnessed on video recordings. It hit home when Tony Robinson, a 19-year-old Black male, was killed by a white police officer in Madison, Wisconsin, triggering massive protests. However, it all boiled over on May 25, 2020, when George Floyd, a 46-year-old Black man, was killed by Derek Chauvin, a 44-year-old white male police officer in the city of Minneapolis. The issue of race, for the first time since the 1960s, was forced into the national conscience. There was an eruption across the nation of protests, riots, demonstrations, and massive groups of people shutting down highways and destroying property. Moreover, the nation was on the precipice of a tumultuous 2020 presidential election. In response to George Floyd and the national conversation about racial injustice, universities, corporations, municipalities, and school districts responded by creating diversity, equity and inclusion (DEI) roles within their organizations, a sign of the growing awareness and engagement with issues of diversity and inclusion.

However, with most movements, there is backlash. The pushback post-George Floyd began with a concerted effort led by Christopher Rufo, who later inspired President Trump and other conservatives to launch an "anti-woke" campaign. Anti-woke is a direct assault on Black history, Black culture, and Black America. The phrase "woke" or "stay woke" was embraced by Black America to replace the standard American English word "awake."

In 1938, Lead Belly wrote the song "Scottsboro Boys," a true story about nine Black American teenage boys who were falsely accused of raping two white women. They served several years in prison for a crime they didn't commit. In the song, Lead Belly sings, "Stay woke." To be "woke" or "stay woke" was a reminder to Black America to stay aware of the dangers of racism, convict leasing, lynchings, and hostile communities when traveling. "Woke" has reemerged several times since the 1930s and simply serves as a crying call to Black America to stay awake. This is part of our history and culture, and to use anti-woke rhetoric can only mean a direct assault on all things Black.

Race and history are ongoing politically hot issues that have led to 18 states signing into law restrictions on the teaching of race. As President Trump was elected to a second term, he launched presidential actions focused on "ending illegal discrimination and restoring merit-based opportunity." Less than two days after being inaugurated, President Trump dismantled DEI departments across the federal government, suspended Black History programs across the federal government, modified the history of the Tuskegee Airmen from the United States Air Force training materials, and will be issuing guidance for states and local school districts to do the same within 120 days of his second term.

In the words of hip-hop pioneer KRS-One, "Why is that?" And what does that mean for the future of a multiracial nation?

Personal Narrative: The 2000s to Present

The first two decades of the new millennium were post-college for me, and I cultivated and nourished a career based on service to young people.

My first job, after graduating from college and moving back to Wisconsin, was working with adjudicated delinquents in the Department of Human Services for Dane County. The young people I primarily worked with were Black youth who were at risk or in the juvenile justice system. Most of my work colleagues were Black, and we were like a family. The Black men were older than me, and I gained so much knowledge about the world over my five-year period working with them. Bobby Austin, in particular, had a library of fantastic literature to which he gave me access, and I embraced all that he was willing to impart. It truly expanded how I see the world. In 2003, I stepped away from working with youth because of Reece Gaines, who is like my little brother. Reece was a first-round pick in the NBA draft. Our parents are close friends and part of the Mount Zion Baptist Church community. Reece and his parents asked me to go with him to help him transition and adjust to the NBA. I did that for his first season with the Orlando Magic, and it was surreal. What I witnessed and experienced in one year behind the scenes of the NBA is another book in itself.

Reece spent one year with the Magic before being traded to the Houston Rockets and then the Milwaukee Bucks. When he was traded to the Rockets, I moved back home and hit rock bottom for the second time because all I had were the clothes on my back and a few thousand dollars in cash. I had to move back home with my parents at 30 years old. But I didn't let this setback define me. I kept pushing forward, applying for jobs daily, determined to rise above my circumstances.

Dr. Richard Harris, whom I mentioned in Chapter 5, informed me of a counseling position at my alma mater, Madison West. I spoke with the principal, whom I knew and deeply respected. He discouraged me from applying for the job, and because of my deep respect for him, I did not apply. Not even one year later, Dr. Harris informed me of the same position at the neighboring high school, Madison Memorial.

I applied and was hired by the late Bruce Dahmen, a tremendous human being and great friend. Before I got rolling in my new position, I was on the second day of my job, and Bruce came into my office and told me I had to go downtown to the central office. I met with the labor relations lawyer, who told me I was terminated. I said, "No, I'm not." She explained that I had not reported an incident they had discovered on my record.

When I was 18, I got a citation for disorderly conduct because my friend got caught stealing. They tried to charge me, too, but I did not have anything. I threw a fit, and they said, "All right, well, we will just give you a disorderly conduct ticket." I went to court, and the judge ordered expungement after one year if I stayed out of trouble. I did not know you had to file a motion and return to court to have it expunged. I thought the disorderly conduct was removed from my record. It had turned up on my record, and I had not reported it.

I tried to explain to the labor relations lawyer that it should not be on my record, but she just looked at me and said, "I cannot do anything for you. You need to go back and clean out your office."

I said, "I cannot stop here," so I went to the human resources director. I tried to plead my case, and he gave me the same answer the labor relations lawyer gave me. I was deflated but not ultimately defeated.

Next, I went to my parents' house and told them what was happening. They told me, "You must figure some things out." So, I met with Pastor Richard Jones, Sr., pastor of Mount Zion Baptist Church at the time. I explained to Pastor Jones what happened, and he called the school district's superintendent. They were literally on the phone for two hours. Jones was putting in work and advocating for a brother, but the superintendent kept saying no. Jones refused to give up and was determined to fight for what he thought was right. Eventually, the superintendent said, "I will give Percy two weeks to get this cleared up." The superintendent ended the meeting by sharing that no employee of MMSD has ever had a termination overturned.

I wasted no time and immediately dug up the case, finding it had been reassigned to a different district attorney. I met with him and said, "Hey, man, I just got a job with the Madison School District. I made a mistake when I was 18, and I'm a changed man. I have not made any mistakes since, and I need this wiped off my record to get my job back." I also explained to the district attorney that it should have been expunged.

He looked at me and said, "I cannot do anything for you."

I asked myself, *Why is everyone closing the door on me?*

Thank God for real friends. I have a good friend and former high school classmate, Joanna, who is a lawyer. I contacted her and told her what was happening, and she went to work for me. Joanna filed a motion and got me in for a hearing within those two weeks. When I went to court, the judge asked me if I wanted to say anything, so I shared a few words. I said that I was trying to do the right thing and that I did not want kids to make the same mistake I had in the past. Too many of my friends fell victim to the traps, and I wanted to do all I could to stop other young brothers and sisters who looked like me from making the same mistakes.

Once I was done speaking, the judge chastised the DA, saying, "I cannot believe you wasted my time. This young man is serving his community, giving back, and doing amazing work." Within 24 hours, it was wiped off my record, and I had my job back.

That was a fight that made me stronger, particularly in my faith. My faith served as my source of strength, supported by my brother, Rev. Richard Jones, Sr. May God rest his soul. Brother Jones passed away in November 2024 as I was editing this chapter. Had I given up, I would not be in the situation I am in today, and I would not have accomplished the things I have. The door had closed on me, but I refused to allow that to be the end of it. So, I got my job back and stayed under Bruce Dahmen's leadership.

As soon as I started rolling in my new position, Bruce took me under his wing and taught me about educational leadership. He encouraged me to get my master's degree in educational leadership because he believed I would be a great principal. I eagerly returned to school in the spring of 2006 to get my teaching license in social studies and a master's degree in educational leadership at Edgewood College. This was a turning point in my career, solidifying my commitment to education and leadership.

I stayed at Memorial for five years as a counselor and coached basketball. Our varsity program was loaded with talent and has won multiple state championships. I was part of the program when Memorial won the state championship in 2009. It was nice to compete for a state championship constantly. However, the absolute satisfaction came from being the academic advisor for several of the players who would earn Division One scholarships. I love the game of basketball and have enjoyed all it has given me, but by this time, I knew my path was to grow in my educational leadership.

I received my master's degree in 2010, and over the next two years, I applied for and interviewed for several leadership positions in the district and fell short each time. While struggling to grow in the district, I pursued opportunities outside the Madison Metropolitan School District. In 2012, I was offered a dean of students position in the Middleton Cross Plains Area School District, a more suburban, affluent, predominantly white school district. I was excited about the new opportunity but left the Madison school district extremely upset. Here I am, a certified Black male educator who was a product of the district, yet I could not grow in the district. At the time I left the district, Black males were the lowest-performing subgroup in the district. It did not make sense to me and left me wondering if the district was committed to improving academic achievement for Black males when they were unwilling to give a home-grown product, who reflected the lowest performing sub-group of students, a shot at leadership.

When I began the dean role, I had additional days added to my contract to help the district with work focused on diversity and the academic performance of Black students. The poor academic performance of Black students in schools throughout Wisconsin is horrific. Across the greater Dane County area in Wisconsin, statistics for Black children and families are the worst in the country. This was highlighted in 2013 when the Wisconsin Council for Children and Families released the Race to Equity Report. The report exposed extreme racial inequalities that were higher than state and national levels.

This was alarming, considering Dane County is known as a progressive and liberal region in Wisconsin. In the current political landscape, there is a perception that liberals are anti-racist and conservatives are racist. If that is true, then why would a progressive community have higher levels of racial inequality than any county in Mississippi, which is conservative and in the South? Based on my personal experiences living in both the North and South, one key difference is that communities in the South confronted racial inequality during the Civil Rights Movement, while many Northern communities did not. Dr. King visited Chicago in the late 1960s and claimed that the racism he encountered there was unlike anything he had experienced in the South. The other stark difference between the two is that in Mississippi, Black people do have some degree of political, economic, and educational infrastructure that they control, and those infrastructures do not exist for Black people in Wisconsin.

The academic data for Black students forced the district to look deeper at its racial disparities. My leadership was growing, and the district was serious about addressing achievement gaps in the district. Therefore, the superintendent allocated funding for a district-level administrator position that empowered me to do the work full-time. Stepping into this newly created role of Director of Equity and Student Achievement felt like a dream come true. I was able to lead and make a positive difference in the lives of Black children and other historically disenfranchised children while ensuring that those students who were already finding success continued to thrive.

I was the only Black leader in the district office when I started the new role. It did not matter because my colleagues and I underwent deep team-building exercises and experiences that created alignment, purpose, and laser-like focus. We were a true team. I always knew that it would take a collective effort, meaning that we would have to work together and find new ways to raise academic achievement, lower behavior referrals and suspensions, and strengthen overall outcomes for all students while focusing on Black students. We did this by accomplishing three things:

1. The district embarked on a journey of shared learning district-wide for several years.
2. We reallocated resources to provide targeted support for Black students and other historically disenfranchised students.
3. We diversified our staff, particularly at the leadership level. As a side note, I always made sure we hired the most qualified person and not someone simply because of the color of their skin. The leaders of color we hired had to go through the same process as other candidates and demonstrate high-quality skills that aligned to what we were looking for.

These were our priority areas, and we started to see an increase in academic achievement for our students who identify as Black or Latino. Graduation rates also began to increase.

The excellent work we were doing as a district went beyond district staff. I was building community partnerships as part of my job duties. I worked with law enforcement, community-based agencies, faith-based organizations, Democrats, and Republicans in Middleton to bring about community-wide learning and increase opportunities and experiences for our students. Community partnerships were essential because they helped fund my annual spring break trips for Black, white, Latino, and Asian students in the district. Because of strong partnerships providing financial support, I was able to take students across the United States of America every year during spring break at a low cost to them. We visited New York City, D.C., Atlanta, and the Deep South of Tennessee, Mississippi, and Louisiana.

In 2014, I rubbed elbows with prominent Republicans in my role as Director of Equity and Student Achievement. Ron Johnson, one of our current U.S. senators, was in Madison to keynote the annual Dane County Lincoln Day dinner that the Republicans have every February. My Republican colleague and good friend, Larry Schulz, who supported the spring break trips financially, invited my wife and me to attend the dinner because I was taking students to Washington, D.C., and he wanted the students to meet Ron Johnson. Larry introduced me to his conservative colleagues, Mike Herl and Kim Babler. They arranged a meeting for me to speak with Senator Johnson to make sure he would meet with my students when we visited Washington.

When we went to dinner, my wife and I met with Ron Johnson in a private room for about 30 minutes. When I worked in Middleton, I took students to see him twice, and each time, he opened up his office and talked to the kids as long as they wanted to talk to him and answered all their questions to the best of his abilities. The other part of the story is I was being vetted and encouraged by Mike Herl and Kim Babler, who at the time were influential Republicans, to consider running for the United States House of Representatives seat in my district. I was shocked and excited, and I thought about it. I decided not to do it because I was enjoying the work in the district.

Over the next several years, my leadership grew beyond the work in Middleton. I started my own consulting firm and have been invited to lecture at Harvard, Teachers College at Columbia, other major universities, churches, community-based organizations, and I have worked closely with dozens of school districts across the nation. Even in the aftermath of George Floyd, with the rise of Black Lives Matter and the push to defund the police, I was contracted out by the Dane County Sheriff's Department to provide professional learning on the history of policing for the entire department of 550-plus staff. Because of the pandemic, I had to present to groups of 15, so I did the same presentation over 30 times. The presentations happened at their training facility, which has gun ranges. When I walked into the presentation room the first day, it was a room full of white officers with heavy tattoos, skull and bone t-shirts with assault rifles, 9mm guns, and ammunition laid out across the tables.

Part of me felt like they were trying to intimidate me, but I remained calm. I started delivering my presentations, and by the third or fourth one, officers were coming up to me before my presentation to share what they heard from their colleagues about it and how they were looking forward to it. My message was laying out the history of policing and how it was designed to be an adversary of Black people and communities. I spoke truth with love; when truth comes in love, people can receive it.

Before the pandemic, I felt confident about the district's

future and what we were doing for all students despite pushback that surfaced near the end of President Trump's first term in the White House. Little did I know that 2020 would be a disastrous year. Kobe Bryant died in a helicopter crash on January 26, 2020, and less than two months later, the school district and others across Dane County closed on Friday, March 13, 2020, as COVID-19 shut down the world for nearly two years. COVID-19 and our increased dependence on technology during the pandemic drastically changed the world.

Millions of students nationwide received virtual learning and connected with friends through social media. When combining time spent on virtual learning, social media apps, and online gaming, it is easy to assume young people were spending at least 12 hours per day on technology during the pandemic. Fortune magazine released a report detailing teens spending almost 8 hours daily on social media and online gaming platforms. Young people spend so much time on technology; it's equivalent to a full-time job. Social media platforms are a hotbed of misinformation, disinformation, and hate speech, to name a few. Online gaming is just as bad when it comes to hate speech.

According to CBS News, eight out of ten gamers have experienced or heard hate speech while gaming online. Excessive use of social media and online gaming is altering the behaviors of our youth. They are becoming further removed from human connection and becoming desensitized. Unbeknownst to most, social media apps and online gaming consoles use algorithms designed to hook users into spending as much time as possible on their platforms to learn everything about the user. While the ultimate goal is to sell your personal information for economic exploitation, the algorithms are working to keep you hooked into their platform by inundating you with information it thinks you like. The algorithms cannot filter fact from fiction when dispersing information to the user. Without critical thinking skills and awareness of how technology influences human behavior, a person will enter an echo chamber. An echo chamber is a space where the user only interacts with people with the same beliefs or opinions. These beliefs are reinforced to a point where alternative perspectives are not considered. This creates the conditions for racist ideology to spread like wildfire, and it does. The evolution of technology and the speed at which it is advancing is scary.

I raise this issue because this past school year (2023-24), I visited over 26 schools in five districts across Wisconsin and California. Most of the schools are predominantly white, both students and staff, and they invited me to meet with and speak to students and staff about the use of hate speech and its negative impact on student learning.

Students across the nation are experiencing an uptick in hate speech and bullying. Most schools are not equipped with the resources or expertise to reduce or eliminate hate speech in schools. I have spoken at school-wide assemblies on hate speech to thousands of students and staff nationwide for several years. Before I talk to students, I always meet with a cross-representation of students to learn about the culture and climate of their school from their perspective. Just last year, I met with hundreds of students across the 26 schools, and the stories are the same for Black students regardless of school district.

Black students are called "niggers," "monkeys," "coons," "cotton pickers," and "chicken munchers," or non-Black students make references to lynching Black people. Black girls have reported that white males have made comments about the desire to rape Black girls as their ancestors did. It is unbelievable that students are using such vitriolic language in 2024. As I gathered qualitative data from my student focus groups, I began to learn from students how much time they spend on technology and how it is influencing their behaviors, and in particular, their normalized use of hate speech. Even adults are spending more time on social media and this is concerning.

Our schools are a microcosm of broader society, and how our students behave also reflects how we act as adults. And how much time are we spending on our devices as adults? Our entire nation has entered into echo chambers, leaving us a nation of tribes. Even our two-party political system has entered echo chambers, which was exacerbated in the summer of 2024. In an unprecedented step, President Joe Biden dropped out of the presidential race and endorsed Vice President Kamala Harris, the first Black female vice president of the United States. What followed on social media was a blitzkrieg of racial insults toward Vice President Harris. Politicians and comedians alike were making derogatory statements about Black people and others leading up to election day, and it seems to be normalized and accepted behavior in our country.

The culture wars and our ever-increasing use of social media are tearing us apart from the highest levels of government all the way down to our local communities and schools. Who will step up in our nation to galvanize a message of unity that resonates with the American people, regardless of political affiliation, race, ethnicity, or creed? Who will emerge as the leader who will prioritize leading with the Preamble to the Constitution as the goal? Who will be the leaders who can help the country establish a set of core values that mirror faith, love, and education? I do not know where we are headed as a nation, but I do know that for over 200 years, my family has stayed true to our core values of faith, love, and education.

My family, who came before me, overcame the period of enslavement and the era of Jim Crow in the Mississippi Delta. Every generation of our existence in America has been one of progress. But more importantly, my family history is one of love for humanity. Even though there were people who intentionally despised them, hated them, discriminated against them, and oppressed them, my family still had love for them. Do we have it in us as a nation to remove ourselves from the echo chambers of social media and find it in our collective souls to have love, empathy, and compassion for one another while respecting different points of view on issues that matter to us?

According to the Constitution, the basic principles of this nation are to establish justice, domestic tranquility, and the promotion of the general welfare for the American people. Do we live in an America where justice, domestic tranquility, and promoting the general welfare are the norm for American citizens irrespective of race? Or do we live in an America that prioritizes technology and profit motives over the people? Dr. King warned us in his "Beyond Vietnam" speech about the time we live in today. I believe the government is incapable of solving our social problems or culture wars. It is up to you and me. *We the people.*

CONCLUSION

*"The Matrix is the world that has been
pulled over your eyes to blind you from the truth."
"There's a difference between knowing the path
and walking the path... Free your mind."*
~ Morpheus (*The Matrix*)

According to the United States Census Bureau, by 2055, the United States will not have a single racial or ethnic majority. Over the next five decades, most of the growth in the United States will be due to new Asian and Hispanic immigration. African immigrants have doubled since 1970, and those who identify as biracial or multiracial have doubled over the past 15 years. Domestic Black Americans, meaning those who have ancestry in the United States dating back to enslavement, make up 12% or approximately 48 million people in the United States. From 2020 to 2060, Black Americans will contribute more than 20% of the total population growth in the United States. Black Americans are also one of the youngest racial groups in the United States, with a median age of 32. That is six years younger than the national average and 11 years younger than white Americans. Consider these demographic shifts and contrast them with the origins of this country and the intentions of the founding fathers for the United States.

The nation is shifting from a predominantly white nation to a multiracial nation. My family is multiracial. I am in an interracial marriage and have a 7-year-old biracial daughter who has already experienced racial and gender harassment. While my wife and I are raising her to be a kind human being to everyone, we are also teaching her to love herself and defend her existence. In two years, we will celebrate the 250th anniversary of the Declaration of Independence. What will this celebration look like? Will we be a unified nation regardless of race, religion, creed, political beliefs, or class? Or will we be further divided along these lines and approaching our own demise as a nation?

In the foreword of Robin DeAngelo's book *White Fragility*, Eric Michael Dyson, a Black American scholar, writes, "Race is a condition. A disease. A card. A plague: Original sin. For much of American history, race has been Black culture's issue; racism, a Black person's burden." Our educational system is partly responsible for the ongoing perpetuation of the racial divide. The American system of education and our media have made us believe that races within humanity are scientific facts. This is not true. Most anthropologists agree that modern humanity began in Africa over 300,000 years ago, and over the past 100,000 years, human beings have migrated out of Africa and populated the earth. If this is true, all of humanity is African, and it is time to course-correct all that we have come to know about ourselves as a species.

Education plays a crucial role in this course correction, as it can help dispel misconceptions about race and promote a more inclusive and accurate understanding of our shared humanity. This is not just a suggestion but a necessity for our future.

In his book *1984*, George Orwell wrote, "Whoever controls the past controls the future. Whoever controls the present controls the past." I love these quotes because they speak to why I wrote this book. The past is our history, and public education is where our nation's history is indoctrinated into our children. What our children learn about world history, United States history, and the history of humanity influences how they perceive the world and see each other. What we teach our young people today is similar to what was taught in the late 1800s in my home state of Wisconsin. A few years ago, I facilitated my signature professional development, "Shifting Mindsets: Teaching and Learning from the Inside Out," to over 80 teachers in a rural conservative school district. During the training, I met a white male social studies teacher whose family history in Wisconsin dates back to the 1800s. He told me he found an elementary geography textbook published in 1883 while rummaging through his family farm. He uses this text in his classroom to teach about the history of race in the United States.

One section states, "There are five races... The Caucasian race or white race is superior to all and exceeds every other race in numbers." It describes the other four races as "Mongolian" (yellow race), "Malay" (brown race), "Ethiopian" (Black race), and "American" (red race). The following section of the text breaks the five races of men into three categories, with the first being "civilized," followed by "half-civilized," and "savage," or "uncivilized." The Malay and Mongolian races were considered half-civilized, while the Blacks and Americans were considered uncivilized and savages. The white race was the only race acknowledged as being civilized.

The curriculum used across most school districts in the United States today is not as explicit and racist as it was in the late 1800s but is still designed to perpetuate the ideology of racial superiority and inferiority between white and Black people. For example, educational reform leader E.D. Hirsch, Jr. wrote a book, *Cultural Literacy,* in 1988. Hirsch propagated in his book that America's students should have a shared body of information while learning to read and write. He coined this shared body of knowledge as "Cultural Literacy," defined as the ability to understand and participate fluently in a given culture. Hirsch believes that young people should learn how to read, write, and effectively communicate by having assumed knowledge about the culture of the United States. Hirsch later founded the Core Knowledge Foundation, and his work has been instrumental in designing the English language arts curriculum for K-12 education that is being taught to millions of students nationwide.

I have examined the Core Knowledge curriculum purchased by textbook and curriculum companies. *Amplify* is an English language arts curriculum that uses the Core Knowledge Foundation's cultural literacy content to teach reading and writing. The content or background knowledge used to teach reading in grades K–5 heavily focuses on history. Students will learn about ancient civilizations around the world except for Africa. The first thing students learn about Black people is their enslavement in the United States as early as first grade. By second grade, students will learn more about the enslavement of Black people in the Civil War unit.

To make matters worse, modifying the units to reflect a more comprehensive history of Black people is difficult because what students learn in each unit is developing background knowledge for future units. Why does the curriculum not include ancient African civilizations? Moreover, why is slavery the first thing that students learn about Black people? What impact might that have on Black children's psychological development and well-being in school? In my professional opinion, it is simply the perpetuation of the racial hierarchy that has existed since colonialism. Hirsch's curriculum does acknowledge immigrants and other cultural minorities in the curriculum; however, it is flawed because it excludes the contributions of ancient African civilizations. The consequences of continuing to mis-educate our young people will have devastating effects in the future.

The way we bring the change we want to see is to ground our efforts in Dr. King's theoretical approach to social change. King's vision for the country and the world was the realization of the Beloved Community. He believed that we could transform the nation into one that was free of racism, gender discrimination, and poverty. He believed that we could someday live together as brothers and sisters. He believed in the power of the human spirit and what is possible if we can connect on the same frequency and vibration of love for one another. His theoretical approach has six guiding principles: information gathering, education, commitment, discussion and negotiation, taking action, and reconciliation. I use these guiding principles in my personal and professional life, intending to live a life where I am genuinely culturally literate. To be truly culturally literate, as defined by the Metiri group, is to have the ability to understand and appreciate your cultural history, values, and norms while embracing and appreciating the cultural history, values, and norms of others.

Our aim as one of the most diverse nations in the world should be to prioritize a path for every American to become culturally literate. The effort must be grassroots and worked from the bottom up. At the local level, it begins with school districts.

Parents and community leaders must question and interrogate what their children learn in their local schools. Pressure must be placed on school districts and state legislatures across the country to change the curriculum to help our students develop the ability to understand and participate fluently in any given culture, regardless of race and ethnicity. Most importantly, we must understand that incorporating diversity of lived experiences and perspectives into what our young people learn creates the conditions for them to develop critical thinking skills and have the ability to coexist in a multiracial world and nation.

The Heritage Foundation, a conservative think tank, has developed Project 2025, a series of policy proposals for an elected conservative president, perhaps President-elect Trump, to restrict teaching so-called "critical race theory" and penalize schools that do so by pulling federal funding. On pages 342-43, Project 2025 states, "By its very design, critical race theory has an 'applied' dimension, as its founders state in their essays that define the theory. Those who subscribe to the theory believe that racism (in this case, treating individuals differently based on race) is appropriate—necessary, even—making the theory more than merely an analytical tool to describe race in public and private life. The theory disrupts America's founding ideals of freedom and opportunity. So, when critical race theory is used as part of school activities such as mandatory affinity groups, teacher training programs in which educators are required to confess their privileges, or school assignments in which students must defend the false idea that America is systemically racist, the theory is actively disrupting the values that hold communities together, such as equality under the law and colorblindness.

- As such, lawmakers should design legislation that prevents the theory from spreading discrimination.

- For K–12 systems under their jurisdiction, federal lawmakers should adopt proposals that say no individual should receive punishment or benefits based on the color of their skin.
- Furthermore, school officials should not require students or teachers to believe that individuals are guilty or responsible for the actions of others based on race or ethnicity."

You cannot teach Black history without teaching about race and racism. These federal policy proposals, if enacted, combined with presidential executive orders dismantling DEI departments and jobs within a month's time across the entire federal government, suspending Black History Month activities, and no longer recognizing Juneteenth and Martin Luther King, Jr. Days are enough actions coming from the federal level to scare school districts into submission. Any effort to teach a more comprehensive history about Black people will die without question. Suppose we do not push back on this. In that case, it further hinders the ability of schools to bring Black and white people together while continuing the perpetuation of Black people as racially inferior.

Moreover, while that fight is necessary, we all must engage in lifelong individual work, regardless of race or ethnicity. The only way we can come together as a people of this nation is to purposefully self-reflect, open our minds to perspective-taking, and live a life that includes cultural immersion experiences that differ from our own. These are evidence-based strategies known to help an individual become culturally literate.

I apply these strategies daily, and they have worked for me. For example, in the months leading up to the presidential election, networks talked about the voting bloc in racial, gender, and geographic terms, to name a few. Regardless of the media outlet, most reporting divides Black and white people politically. The rhetoric is always that Democrats are the party for Black people and Republicans are the party for white people. It is fascinating to me how working-class Black Americans from urban and suburban communities vote Democrat while rural, working-class white Americans vote Republican. I have spent time in urban and suburban communities across the nation and have worked in several predominantly white rural school districts across the nation. Both communities have under-resourced schools for their children's education and share many of the same economic struggles. The only difference is their location and race, yet neither community is aware of their shared problem because they are never in community with one another. Our inability to come together is shameful, given the fact that we have lived in the same nation together for centuries.

From my own experiences, I believe both communities share common ground. I have connected with and established relationships with rural white Americans because we share similar values, such as family, faith, hard work, and education. The only way we can find common ground is to unplug from technology and the media, sit down together with an open mind, and engage in healthy and courageous conversations about what we want for our children, bread-and-butter issues, and the future. If we can set the table in love and bring people together on the issues I mentioned, there's only one step left for us to transform our nation.

The last step for every American is to have faith and love for one another. Our faith must be rooted in truth. According to Merriam-Webster's Dictionary, faith is defined in three ways: "allegiance to duty or person," "belief and trust in and loyalty to God," and "something that is believed, especially with strong conviction." As a man of God, I fully embrace the spiritual definition of faith and call on all people of all religions to find ways to become ecumenical and not allow religious doctrine and theology to continue to divide faith-based communities. Moreover, for all Americans, regardless of spiritual beliefs, we must have allegiance to each other as citizens and not political parties. As a nation, we must undergo a "radical revolution of values." We need a common set of values that guide who we are as a nation. I offer faith as defined by Merriam-Webster's Dictionary, love, and education. These have worked for me and my family, and I believe they can be embraced by us all, irrespective of race.

And in this moment in time, I am personally confronted with the reality that the powers that be are aggressively working to bring my career and life's work to an end. I guess it is fitting that this book is coming out when it is because the powers that be can't stop it from reaching the people. This book is my legacy. It is a story I am sharing for others to tell. It is leaving my impression on the next generation. It is not a story comprised of how to make money or accumulate material things, but a story of character, conviction, and compassion.

As a man of compassion and despite my uncomfortable reality, I pray that President Trump delivers on his promise to usher in a golden age, which means a period of peace, harmony, stability, and prosperity. I pray that President Trump delivers on his promise to make Dr. King's dream a reality. I pray that we remind ourselves of the nation's motto, *"E pluribus unum,"* a Latin phrase meaning "out of many, one." I pray that we remind ourselves that justice, domestic tranquility, and the promotion of the general welfare are coded in the Preamble to the Constitution. I pray that we remind ourselves that faith without work is dead. We the people have to do the work to become "out of many, one." And given where we are today, it won't be easy, but it can be done. I believe in the power of faith, love, and education. I believe if we embrace faith, love, and education as a set of common values, we will become one out of many. I love America. I love you. May God bless the United States of America!

Peace and love.

SELF REFLECTIVE ACTIVITIES

Adapted from *Autoethnography as Method* by Heewon Chang

1. Create a CultureGram® that outlines your gender, race/ethnicity, nationality, language(s), religion, socio-economic status, level of education, profession, and interests. Explain three primary identities you selected and your reasons for these selections. Reflect on and write what you have learned about yourself through culturegramming.
2. Create your family tree and include all or some key family members who have meaningfully contributed to the shaping of your life. Your family tree doesn't have to include everyone in your family. Describe your family according to your tree and add details about individuals included in it.
3. List five personal, familial, or social rituals, in order of importance, in which you have participated. Briefly describe the context of each ritual. Select the most

important one and describe it in detail in terms of who, when, where, what, and how. Explain why it is important in your life.

4. List five artifacts, in order of importance, that represent your culture and briefly describe what each artifact represents. Select one and expound on the cultural meaning of this article to your life.
5. Select a place of significance that helped you gain an understanding of yourself and your relationship to others. Draw the place, putting in as many details as possible. You may outline the place or do a realistic drawing. Identify objects and persons in the drawing when necessary. Expand this exercise to additional places. Describe the place and explain why this place is significant to you.
6. List five values, in order of importance, that you consider important in your life. Give a brief definition of each in your own words. Select the most important one and explain why it is important.
7. When you have completed reading this book, draw a Venn diagram to show similarities and differences between your life and mine. Select one similarity and difference from your diagram and describe in detail how you and I are similar to and different from each other. Reflect on and analyze what you have discovered about your culture in the process. And if we were able to meet each other in person, how might you leverage what we have in common to begin building an authentic relationship between the two of us?

THANK YOU FOR READING MY BOOK!

Download Your Free Gifts

Just to say thanks for buying and reading my book, I would like to give you access to valuable resources and an invitation to free virtual talkbacks with me!

To Download, Scan the QR Code:

I appreciate your interest in my book and value your feedback as it helps me improve future versions of this book. I would appreciate it if you could leave your invaluable review on Amazon.com with your feedback. Thank you!

www.ingramcontent.com/pod-product-compliance
Lightning Source LLC
Chambersburg PA
CBHW031259110426
42743CB00041B/762